T0220218

Windows To Go

A Guide for Users and IT Professionals

Joli Ballew

Apress®

Windows To Go

Joli Ballew
Garland, Texas
USA

ISBN-13 (pbk): 978-1-4842-2133-4   ISBN-13 (electronic): 978-1-4842-2134-1
DOI 10.1007/978-1-4842-2134-1

Library of Congress Control Number: 2016949069

Managing Director: Welmoed Spahr
Acquisitions Editor: Gwenan Spearing
Development Editor: Laura Berendson
Technical Reviewer: Massimo Nardone
Editorial Board: Steve Anglin, Pramila Balen, Aaron Black, Laura Berendson, Louise Corrigan,
    Jonathan Gennick, Celestin Suresh John, Nikhil Karkal, Robert Hutchinson,
    James Markham, Susan McDermott, Matthew Moodie, Natalie Pao, Gwenan Spearing
Coordinating Editor: Nancy Chen
Copy Editor: Lori Jacobs
Compositor: SPi Global
Indexer: SPi Global
Cover Image: Designed by freepik.com

Distributed to the book trade worldwide by Springer Science+Business Media New York, 233 Spring Street, 6th Floor, New York, NY 10013. Phone 1-800-SPRINGER, fax (201) 348-4505, e-mail orders-ny@springer-sbm.com, or visit www.springer.com. Apress Media, LLC is a California LLC and the sole member (owner) is Springer Science + Business Media Finance Inc (SSBM Finance Inc). SSBM Finance Inc is a Delaware corporation.

For information on translations, please e-mail rights@apress.com, or visit www.apress.com.

Apress and friends of ED books may be purchased in bulk for academic, corporate, or promotional use. eBook versions and licenses are also available for most titles. For more information, reference our Special Bulk Sales–eBook Licensing web page at www.apress.com/bulk-sales.

Any source code or other supplementary materials referenced by the author in this text is available to readers at www.apress.com/. For detailed information about how to locate your book's source code, go to www.apress.com/source-code/.

Printed on acid-free paper

*For Teresa, my best friend and confidant, thank your for
coming into my life and staying there.*

Contents at a Glance

Contents

About the Author

Joli Ballew is a Microsoft MVP and Windows expert. She has written almost 60 books, most on Windows technologies. She currently works at Lynda.com authoring and filming training videos, is an adjunct professor of technology at Brookhaven College in Farmers Branch, Texas, and teaches Microsoft certification boot camps at Collin College in Plano, Texas. Joli spends her spare time doing yoga and running and spending time with her family.

About the Technical Reviewer

Massimo Nardone has more than 22 years of experience in Security, Web/Mobile development, and Cloud and IT architecture. His true IT passions are Security and Android. He has been programming and teaching how to program with Android, Perl, PHP, Java, VB, Python, C/C++, and MySQL for more than 20 years.

He holds a Master of Science degree in Computing Science from the University of Salerno, Italy. He has worked as a Project Manager, Software Engineer, Research Engineer, Chief Security Architect, Information Security Manager, PCI/SCADA Auditor, and Senior Lead IT Security/Cloud/SCADA Architect for many years.

His technical skills include Security, Android, Cloud, Java, MySQL, Drupal, Cobol, Perl, Web and Mobile development, MongoDB, D3, Joomla, Couchbase, C/C++, WebGL, Python, Pro Rails, Django CMS, Jekyll, Scratch, etc.

He currently works as Chief Information Security Officer (CISO) for Cargotec Oyj. He worked as visiting lecturer and supervisor for exercises at the Networking Laboratory of the Helsinki University of Technology (Aalto University). He holds four international patents (PKI, SIP, SAML, and Proxy areas). Massimo has reviewed more than 40 IT books for different publishing companies and he is the coauthor of *Pro Android Games* (Apress, 2015).

Acknowledgments

Thank you to everyone at Apress for the opportunity to write this book, including but not limited to Gwenan Spearing, Melissa Maldonado, and Nancy Chen, with a special thanks to Ed Liberman for introducing me to the folks here. I've enjoyed working with everyone. I'd also like to thank my family for their support. My daughter and her family are my rock and foundation. My roommate and her family are my local support and go out of their way to make sure I'm able to work when I need to. Of course, I'd like to thank my agent at Studio B Literary Agency, Stacey Czarnowski, who is always looking out for me and my best interests.

CHAPTER 1

■ ■ ■

Introducing Windows To Go

Employees are becoming more and more mobile. On the road, they often work from personal devices, in a Bring Your Own Device (BYOD) to work scenario. They might use company-provisioned laptops as well, and from home they may connect remotely to corporate desktop PCs. In these scenarios and others they connect through virtual private networks (VPNs) and virtual desktops. Beyond that, though, some users, while on company property, are required to roam from workstation to workstation to do their jobs. In the former situation, employees often have their own computers, laptops, or mobile devices. When users do have to roam from PC to PC, they often log in to a domain and have access to a roaming user profile to make their computing experience the same no matter which computer they log onto. There are other scenarios though where these types of solutions won't work, and other solutions are required.

As an example, there are instances where certain employees aren't assigned a specific computer, even when they are on company property. They might connect using a Virtual Private Network (VPN) or through the cloud. They can also use Windows To Go. Whatever the case, they need to access an operating system. Some users must have access to an operating system when in remote offices, even when they can't or don't have the ability to employ a laptop or other mobile device. Users might be consultants, too, and simply not have the authorization required to access a machine in an enterprise, although guest machines might be available for those contract workers. All of these scenarios, as well as others, present a problem for network administrators. These users need access to an operating system even when a personal computing device isn't available. This is where Windows To Go comes in.

Windows To Go offers a way for mobile, corporate employees to work more efficiently by enabling them to access a personalized Windows workspace from any Windows-based PC that meets Windows To Go host requirements. These workspaces, which users carry with them, are stored on portable USB drives, and the users simply insert the drive and boot the PC to gain access. Of course, the host PC must be able to boot to the device, but most can be configured to do that without much effort.

■ **Tip** It's important to note that Windows To Go is not meant to replace desktops, laptops, or other mobile devices, but equally important to understand is that it can provide an alternate workplace option when one is required. You'll learn the pros and cons of when you'd opt to use Wiindows to Go as a solution (and when you wouldn't) as you read through this book.

© Joli Ballew 2016
J. Ballew, *Windows To Go*, DOI 10.1007/978-1-4842-2134-1_1

Getting Started with Windows To Go

Network administrators create Windows To Go workspaces using the Windows To Go Creator from Windows 8, 8.1, and 10 Enterprise machines. Although many types of computers can serve as hosts, only Enterprise machines can be used to create Windows To Go drives. If you aren't already aware, these versions of the Windows operating systems can only be acquired by corporations and enterprises that have signed on with Microsoft's Volume Licensing agreement. Windows 8, 8.1, and 10 Enterprise are not available for download or on DVD to the general public.

For those companies that do opt for the Enterprise release and decide to provision USB drives to their employees, there is the option to customize the Windows image to match the needs of the environment. Network administrators can add device drivers, software packages like Microsoft Office, third-party products like Adobe Reader, proprietary applications, and they can even customize desktop backgrounds and screensavers, among other things. Larger corporations might have multiple images, one for each department or project group.

With regard to security, administrators can enable Bitlocker to protect the drives they commission with a password. I'll suggest you always do that. If the drive is lost or stolen, it can't be used without this information. Also, because all that's physically lost is a USB drive, the cost of replacement is low. Reimaging a USB drive if it becomes corrupt is just as easy as making one as well, making Windows To Go an affordable and easy-to-manage alternative for those businesses that can use it. Figure 1-1 shows the Windows To Go Creator on a Windows 10 Enterprise computer.

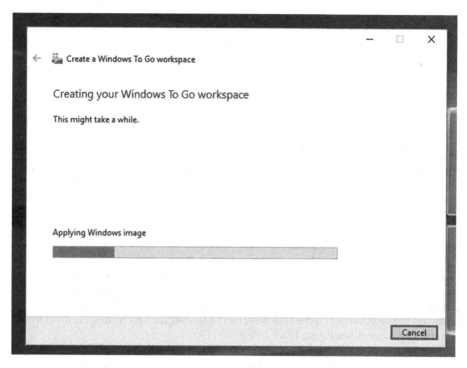

Figure 1-1. *The Windows To Go Creator is a wizard-based application. Use it to create Windows To Go drives.*

■ **Note**   Windows To Go workspaces (USB drives) can only be created from Windows 8-based and Windows 10 Enterprise computers.

The Differences Between Windows To Go and a Typical Windows Installation

For the end user, the Windows To Go experience is very similar to the "regular" Windows experience. It doesn't matter how you achieve that experience; the user can run Windows on a desktop or laptop computer, or even from a pool of available virtual desktops in a domain. However, Windows To Go is not a replacement for an operating system in the long term, and there are limitations to what it can provide. Here are a few items to consider, at least in terms of an employee's standpoint:

- The host computer's internal disks are offline

- Trusted Platform Module (TPM) isn't used (Trusted Boot can be)

- Hibernation is disabled by default

3

- Windows Recovery Environment (RE) isn't available

- The Store is available but with limitations

- Users can roam from computer to computer with a single Windows To Go drive

Let's take a look at each of these items in more detail.

Internal Disks Are Offline

First, note that internal disks are offline. This means that the host computer's data can't be accessed by the Windows To Go user. Likewise, when a Windows To Go drive is inserted into a system while that system is running, the Windows To Go drive will not be listed in Windows Explorer.

TPM Can't Be Used

In addition, a TPM chip can't be used. That's because TPM chips are associated with a single computer, and Windows To Go users access multiple systems. Because of this, BitLocker is used in its place. BitLocker Drive Encryption requires the user to input a password before Windows on the USB drive can be loaded, thus protecting the drive from unauthorized access. See Figure 1-2.

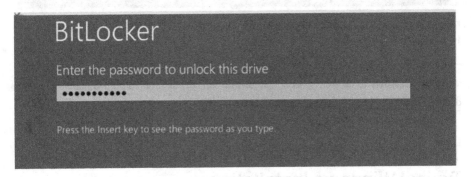

Figure 1-2. *BitLocker Drive Encryption protects the Windows To Go drive by requiring a password*

Hibernation and Sleep Considerations

Hibernation is disabled by default to make sure that the Windows To Go workspace can be moved from computer to computer easily. Hibernation could slow down the process of removing the drive when the user is finished working. It's possible to enable hibernation using Group Policy settings though.

There are additional Group Policy settings to consider, including modifying standby sleep states on the host PC when the computer has booted to a Windows To Go workspace. Sleep states could make the Windows To Go user think that the computer has shut down, when in reality it's only sleeping, and that user may simply remove his or her USB drive. When a USB workspace is removed without going through the proper shut-down procedures it's possible for the drive to become corrupt. It's possible that harm could come to the host computer as well. If you enable this policy setting (**Disallow standby sleep states (S1-S3) when starting from a Windows To Go workspace**), the Windows To Go workspace cannot use the standby states to cause the PC to enter sleep mode.

Windows Recovery Environment Is Not Available

The next item to understand is that the Windows RE isn't available to the end user. There's no way to refresh or reset a Windows To Go drive. In cases where this is required, you should reimage the drive. This is because resetting to some manufacturer standard simply doesn't work for a Windows To Go workspace. Thus, Windows RE is disabled.

Using the Windows Store

The Windows Store behavior differs somewhat for end users running Windows 8-based machines, depending on what operating system is on their Windows To Go drives. For those users with Windows 8.1, there is no difference; store apps can roam between multiple PCs. With Windows 8, the Windows Store is disabled by default. This has to do with how apps are licensed through the store and how they are associated with specific hardware. Through Group Policy though, the Windows Store can be enabled for a Windows To Go workspace for a single PC and Store apps can be used on that workspace.

Roaming with Windows To Go

■ **Note** When creating Windows To Go images, make sure the image contains all of the device drivers that could possibly be required by host PCs. You'll learn about the requirements and the process for making images in various chapters in this book.

Finally, users can roam with Windows To Go. Windows To Go drives can be booted on multiple computers, as you know, but how this works is complex. Briefly, and there will be more in Chapter 2, when a Windows To Go workspace is initially booted, that workspace detects all of the hardware on that host PC and loads the necessary drivers. The next time the same host is used, those drivers are ready and installed, and the host is identified easily.

■ **Caution** The applications that you want to add to the Windows To Go image (and workspace) need to support roaming. Some applications are bound to hardware and can cause problems when used on another machine.

Hardware Requirements

Both the host and the USB drive must meet hardware requirements. USB drives must be "Windows To Go Certified" and host PCs must meet hardware, BIOS, boot, and architectural specifications among other things. When planning a Windows To Go deployment, hardware is of the utmost importance and one of the first areas to consider.

For end users, though, understand that their biggest concern and opportunity for failure is the actual process of booting to the device. You will give them a compatible USB drive, but in the end, the user is responsible for booting up the drive. Due to the nature of the process, differing firmware, BIOS settings, and so on, the boot process can go awry in many ways. Thus, it's important to understand and possibly even educate your own users on how the boot process works, at least with regard to selecting compatible machines.

Selecting the USB Drives

The USB drives you select for Windows To Go workspaces must meet specific requirements. There is no specific brand or size that I will suggest, as the available options change as time passes and technology evolves. When purchasing these drives, though, make sure they are Windows To Go Certified; that's all you need to do. Here's what "certified" means, in a nutshell:

- The drives are built specifically for high read and write speeds. They support thousands of random access input and output operation per second. The faster these specs are, the better Windows To Go will run.

- Certified drives are built to ensure they will boot and run on host hardware that meet host requirements put in place by Microsoft. Host requirements are detailed next, but they must run a compatible version of Windows 7, 8, or 10.

- Drives must be backed with a manufacturer warranty and should be built to last.

Selecting the Host PC

As with selecting USB drives to hold Windows To Go, you must select hosts that support it. Like USB drives, hosts go through a certification process as well. That process requires that the host run a compatible version of Windows 7, Windows 8, or Windows 10. Windows RT won't work, and Windows To Go can't be used on Mac computers.

Beyond that, there are a few other things to understand about the host PC. First, the host computer must be capable of booting to a USB drive and USB boot up must be enabled. PCs that are certified for use with Windows 7 or later are capable of this, but settings might need to be changed in BIOS. There is a Windows To Go setting where administrators can enable this as well, as shown in Figure 1-3. To find this, simply type Windows To Go at a Windows 8-based Start screen or search for it in the Windows 10 search box on the Taskbar, then click Change Windows To Go Startup Options. If you're using a Windows 7 host, you'll want to take a look at the BIOS settings during startup. I usually opt for the newest and best machine I can find, which is often one running Windows 10. However, any compatible computer will do, provided it meets the requirements listed.

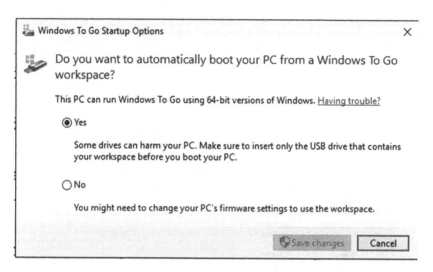

Figure 1-3. Allow a computer to boot to a Windows To Go device using the graphical interface available in Windows

You'll learn more about the processor requirements next, but for now note that the processor architecture must support the image on the Windows To Go drive. The processor must be 1 GHz or faster, and there must be at least 2 GB of Random Access Memory (RAM). DirectX9 graphics card with WDDM 1.2 or greater must also be installed in the machine.

Checking Architectural Compatibility

As noted earlier, the image on the Windows To Go drive needs to be compatible with the architecture of the host PC. Firmware must be compatible too. Table 1-1 shows the various scenarios and host PC requirements.

Table 1-1. Checking Architectural Compatiblity Between the Host and the Windows To Go Drive

Host	Host Processor	Windows To Go Image
Legacy BIOS	32-bit	32-bit
Legacy BIOS	64-bit	32-bit and 64-bit
UEFI BIOS	32-bit	32-bit
UEFI BIOS	64-bit	64-bit

7

One way to see the host processor's specifications is to right-click This PC (on a Windows 10 machine) and click Properties. This opens the System window from Control Panel. There are multiple ways to get to this window from Windows 10 and other operating system versions. Once there, note what is available next to System Type. Figure 1-4 shows this PC is running a 64-bit operating system with an x-64 based processor. This host is also UEFI, so it can support a 64-bit Windows To Go image.

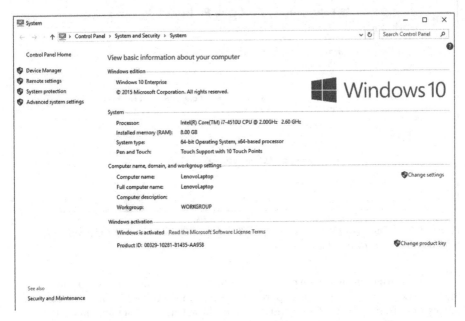

Figure 1-4. *Discover the host's architectural specifications in the System window*

Tips for Configuring the BIOS

If you're sure you have a compatible host, and you want that host always to be able to boot to an inserted Windows To Go drive, for Windows 8 and up, use the Startup Options shown in Figure 1-3 to configure it. If you are using a Windows 7 machine or only want to allow the Windows To Go drive one time, you should make the change in the BIOS.

How you configure the BIOS isn't the same for all computers. The manufacturer determines the method you'll use to get into the settings and involves pressing a specific key during the normal startup process. That key could be F2, F9, F10, F12, or something else. Here are a few of the major manufacturer's settings (although things can and do change):

- Acer

  - BIOS F2

  - Boot Menu F12

- ASUS
  - Bios DEL
  - Boot Menu N/A
- Dell
  - BIOS F2
  - Boot Menu F12
- Hewlett Packard
  - BIOS F10
  - Boot Menu F9
- Lenovo
  - BIOS F2
  - Boot Menu F12
- Samsung
  - BIOS F2
  - Boot Menu F10

Summary

As users become more mobile it's important to offer them a way to access an operating system while away from their own desktop or laptop. Windows To Go offers a way for these users to work in these scenarios and others by providing them with a personalized Windows workspace, which they can access from any compatible Windows-based PC. Windows To Go workspaces can be configured to meet any company's needs and the image on them can be modified and personalized in hundreds of ways. These workspaces are stored on portable USB drives that users can take with them. In this chapter you learned what is required of both the physical drive that the workspace that it is configured to use, as well as the host that the drive is booted with.

In Chapter 2 you'll learn how end users work with Windows To Go. You'll learn more about the boot process, how to sign in, how to navigate Windows, and how to access resources, among other things.

CHAPTER 2

■ ■ ■

Using Windows To Go

In Chapter 1 you learned quite a bit about Windows To Go, including the differences between a traditional installation of Windows and Windows running on a USB drive. You learned what is required of the host computer, which must meet specific certification requirements for both hardware and software. You learned that processor architecture has to match between the host and the Windows To Go drive, and that limitations exist with regard to the Windows Store for Windows 8 and access to local resources (specifically the host's internal hard drive) for all operating systems. In this chapter we'll continue along that same path, keeping a focus on the end user and getting started with Windows To Go from an end-user perspective, including what problems can arise for them. Let's look once more at the reasons an enterprise would employ Windows To Go before we get started, and let's look at a few other ways you could use Windows To Go that you may not have thought of.

Additional Thoughts on Windows To Go

In a nutshell, Windows To Go offers users the ability to roam from machine to machine or building to building while maintaining access to an operating system, all without having to carry a laptop or tablet with them. All they need is access to a compatible PC running a compatible operating system. Companies can put their own image on a Windows To Go drive, and can easily replicate, provision, replace, and otherwise manage the drives once a system is put into place. Windows To Go is stored on a USB stick and protected by BitLocker, so loss is more easily handled monetarily when things go awry versus what happens when a user misplaces, damages, or otherwise loses a laptop. It can also be used to share PCs. In addition, traveling with a USB drive instead of other mobile hardware lets users travel lighter.

Beyond this, at least with regard to how you'd use Windows To Go, there are a few things that you might not have considered when thinking about Windows To Go. For instance, think about how Windows To Go could be used in a classroom setting or as a corporate training tool. Instructors can give students access to an operating system that they can work with and on while in class, and then take home with them to continue their studies when class is over. In many scenarios, there would be no need to set up a lab or have specialized software. In any training setting, users can move around easily, and can sit at any workstation they like, facilitating small group work and similar scenarios.

© Joli Ballew 2016

J. Ballew, *Windows To Go*, DOI 10.1007/978-1-4842-2134-1_2

Additionally, think about how users in larger companies with domains could use Windows To Go effectively, specifically to access the domain when required. Although they could save to an external storage medium, like Dropbox or OneDrive, it is possible to direct users to save on the actual domain servers. In this instance, users are supplied with direct access to domain resources with a feature called DirectAccess. DirectAccess is only one of the ways Windows To Go users can work from a Windows To Go workspace and still maintain a corporate identity and be managed by administrators.

Finally, having a Windows To Go workspace in highly volatile environments, or those that simply aren't stable, enables users to get back to work quickly should their own laptops or PCs encounter problems. Getting users back to work quickly, perhaps even in a lab setting, enables them to work more efficiently. Of course, users could work inside their Windows To Go workspace from home and not have to worry much about how those systems work or how they should save data when necessary.

■ **Caution** Remember that Windows To Go isn't always the best solution in many situations. It can't be used in USB hubs, you should always enable Bitlocker, and it isn't a long-term solution.

Creating a Basic Windows To Go Workspace

In this chapter you'll start by building your own Windows To Go workspace that you can experiment with. Later in this book you'll learn how network administrators do it using other tools, and how they create unique images and deploy workspaces to users, among other things. For now though, just having your own personal Windows To Go stick is a good place to start.

To create your own Windows To Go workspace you'll need a few things. First, you'll need a USB drive that is certified for Windows To Go use. When shopping for this drive, look for the appropriate labeling that defines it as such prior to the purchase. You should see something like what's shown in Figure 2-1, which specifically states that it supports Windows To Go.

- Capacity: 64 GB
- Interface: USB 3.0
- NAND Flash: MLC
- Sequential Read: 320 MB/s
- Sequential Write: 120 MB/s
- OS Support: Windows 8/7/Vista/XP, Windows To Go, and OS X

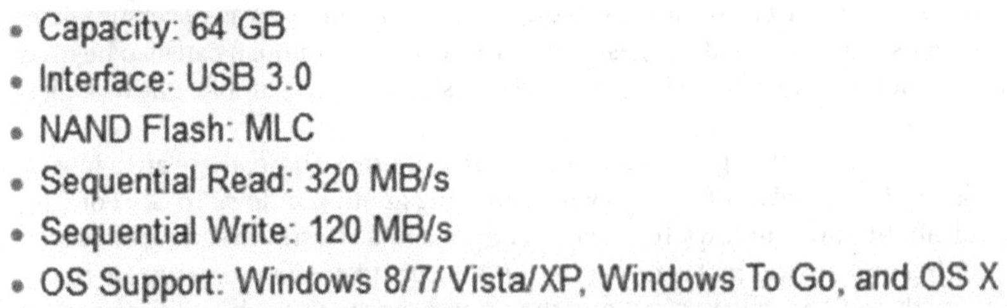

Figure 2-1. Choose a USB drive that specifically states that it supports Windows To Go. There are many manufacturers that make these drives as well as those that are already installed with Windows To Go.

With that in hand, you'll need to acquire a copy of Windows 8, 8.1, or 10 Enterprise and install it on a computer, perhaps in a lab setting but, at least for now, on something other than a production machine. You don't have to join a domain to get started here either, although you can should you desire. You will need administrator privileges once you have an Enterprise version of Windows installed, up, and running. Finally, you'll need a genuine copy of the operating system you want to place on the Windows To Go drive, complete with a valid license. Once that's all in order, continue here.

■ **Note** Once you've placed an operating system on a Windows To Go drive and created the workspace, you can't upgrade that system. If you want to put a different operating system on the drive, you'll have to reimage it.

When you're ready, log on to your Windows Enterprise machine. From here you'll access the Windows To Go Creator and create your first Windows To Go workspace. Here are the steps:

1. Sign in with administrator privileges to a Windows 8, 8.1, or 10 Enterprise PC.

2. Locate a copy of the operating system you want to use for Windows To Go, and place the .wim file on the PC, a network share, USB drive, or DVD, or otherwise make it accessible.

3. Locate the product identification number associated with the Windows image you want to use, as applicable.

WHERE TO ACQUIRE WINDOWS ENTERPRISE

Windows Enterprise isn't available from a box store, and you can't simply buy a copy of it from Microsoft either. Windows Enterprise is available through a volume licensing agreement from Microsoft or with a subscription to Microsoft Developer Network (MSDN). This means it is generally used for professional purposes in larger organizations, but that doesn't mean it can't be used elsewhere and in other situations.

Additionally, the Community Technology Preview (CTP) of Service Pack 1 for System Center 2012 Configuration Manager includes support for user self-provisioning of Windows To Go drives. You can download an evaluation copy of Configuration Manager 2012 SP1 CTP from the Microsoft Download Center.

■ **Caution**   The USB drive you use should already be initialized and a volume created on it prior to provisioning the drive with Windows To Go. If you aren't sure if your drive is or is not initialized, it likely is. Go ahead and try to run the wizard and address the situation only if the need arises.

---

4.   Insert the Windows To Go Certified USB drive you purchased into a USB 2.0 or higher port on the Windows Enterprise machine.

5.   Search for Windows To Go from a search window and in the results select Windows To Go Creator Wizard. If you don't see this as an option:

a.   Open Control Panel.

b.   Change from Category to Large Icons, if applicable.

c.   Click Windows To Go. See Figure 2-2.

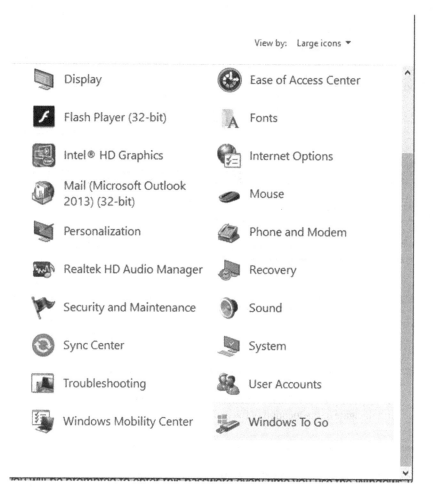

Figure 2-2. *If the Windows To Go Creator doesn't appear in the results list after searching for Windows To Go, open it from Control Panel*

6. If applicable, in the User Account Control dialog box, confirm you want to use this program.

7. When prompted to choose the USB drive you'd like to use for Windows To Go, select the drive and then click Next. If you encounter errors, as shown in Figure 2-3, you'll need to correct them.

15

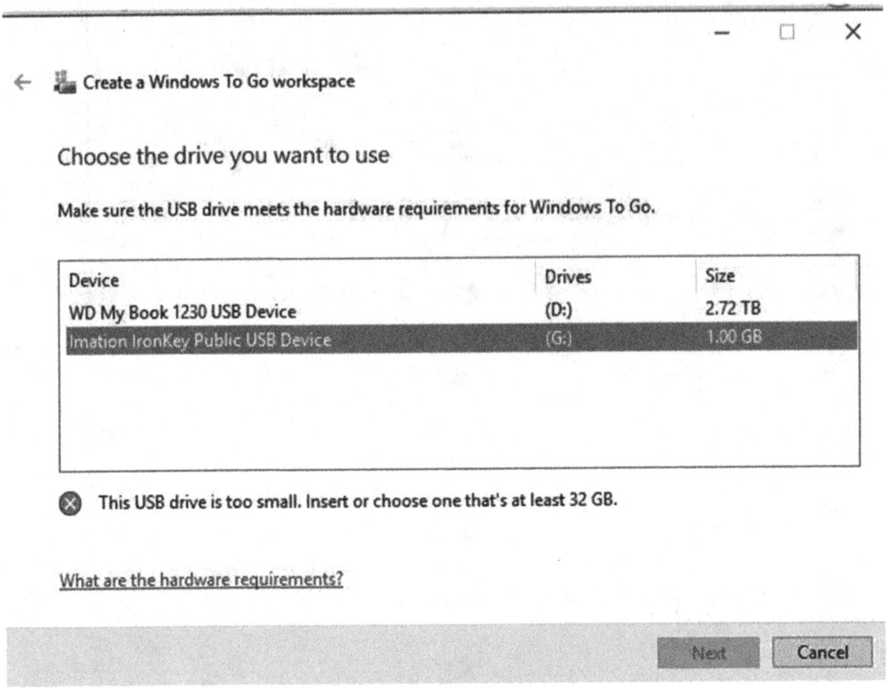

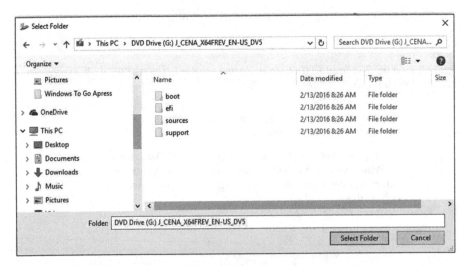

Figure 2-3. Resolve any issues that arise during the selection process

8. When prompted to choose an image, click Add Search Location and navigate to the location of the .wim file. See Figure 2-4.

Figure 2-4. Select the .wim file to use for the Windows To Go drive

9. Click Select Folder.

10. Click the file name and click Next.

11. On the optional Set a BitLocker password page, select Use BitLocker with my Windows To Go Workspace. See Figure 2-5. I recommend you do this.

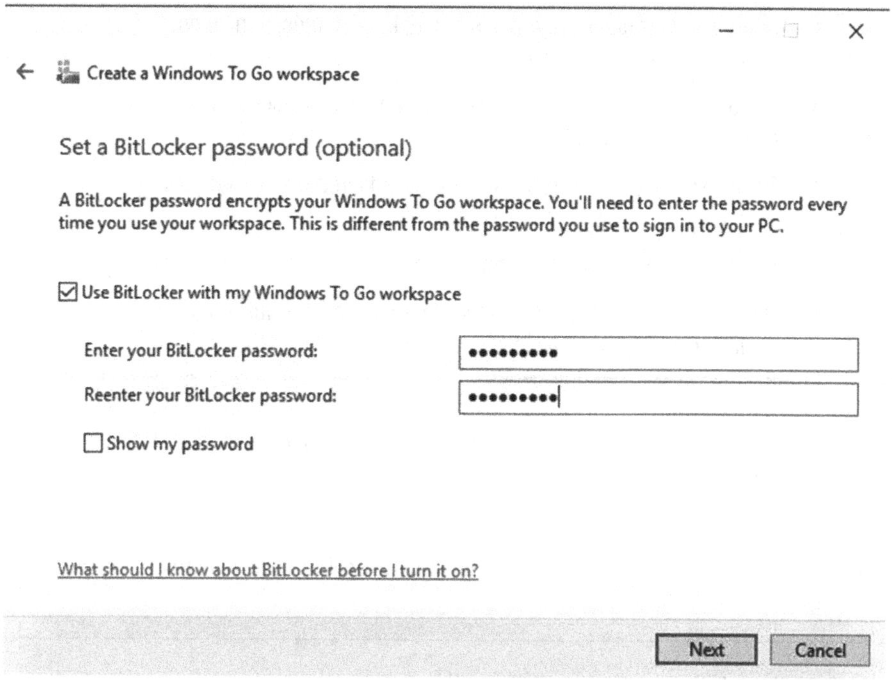

← ▦ Create a Windows To Go workspace — ◻ ✕

Set a BitLocker password (optional)

A BitLocker password encrypts your Windows To Go workspace. You'll need to enter the password every time you use your workspace. This is different from the password you use to sign in to your PC.

☑ Use BitLocker with my Windows To Go workspace

Enter your BitLocker password: ●●●●●●●●●

Reenter your BitLocker password: ●●●●●●●●●|

☐ Show my password

What should I know about BitLocker before I turn it on?

| Next | Cancel |

Figure 2-5. Create a BitLocker password during the Windows To Go creation process

12. Type a password and enter it again to confirm.

■ **Note**   DiskPart is a command-line tool that you can use to manually partition removable media such as flash drives. If you want to perform advanced partitioning functions with a USB drive, consider reading about DiskPart here before you start.

BEST PRACTICES: PASSWORDS

Keep this in mind when creating passwords:

- Use a combination of words, symbols, numbers, and upper- and lower-case letters.

- Don't use your name, your dog's name, kids' names, and so on. Avoid words like "Password" and "User."

- Avoid including personal information such as social security numbers or addresses.

- Try to use made-up words, and avoid words in the dictionary. An example of such would be ILuvCatz54!x.

- Avoid consecutive numbers and letters.

- Don't use a password you use for other places, like web sites, e-mail accounts, bank accounts, and so on.

13. Wait for the process to complete, which could take up to 30 minutes.

■ **Note** Using BitLocker to encrypt your Windows To Go USB drive will protect the drive with a password, also called a key.

14. Configure the Windows To Go startup options as desired.

15. Once completed click Yes or No to boot to the new drive now or to wait. See Figure 2-6.

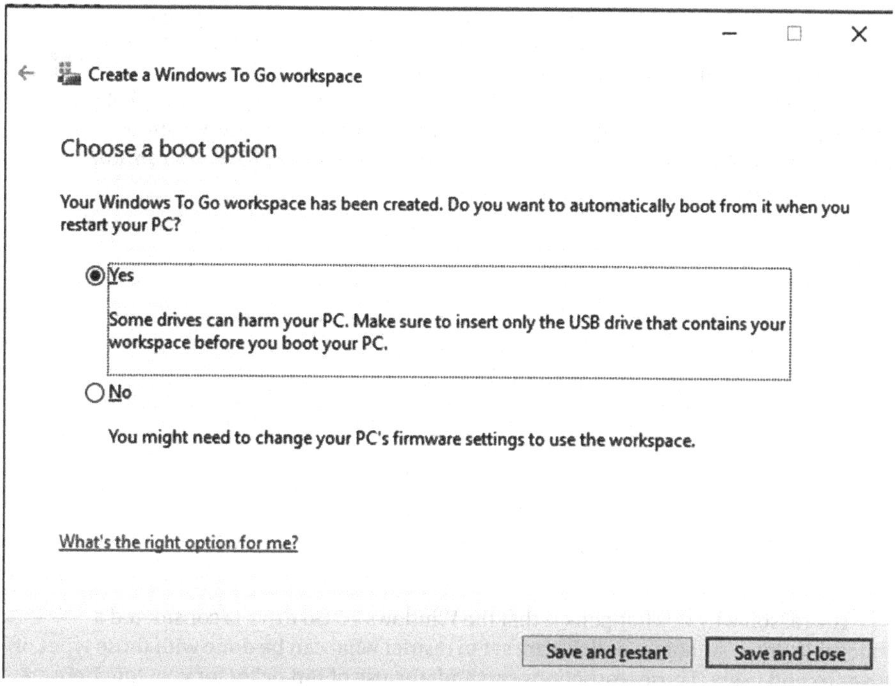

Figure 2-6. *At the end of the process, choose whether or not to boot to the drive now or wait*

16.   Click Save and Restart or Save and Close, as desired.

■ **Note**   The first time you boot to the Windows To Go drive you'll be prompted to set up Windows, just as you would with any brand-new operating system. You might want to do that before giving the drive to an end user. Unless you're using an Enterprise image, you'll also be prompted to input a product ID. In all instances you'll need to activate the operating system.

Troubleshooting BitLocker in the Windows To Go Creation Process

Like anything, there are several reasons why the Windows To Go creation process could fail. As noted in the first few steps of the tutorial, sometimes the Windows To Go Creator wizard simply won't appear in the search results. As noted, in this instance you can open the wizard from Control Panel using one of the other icon views. It's also possible that the USB drive you've selected isn't compatible for one reason or another. You saw this in Figure 2-3. Perhaps it's not a large enough drive or isn't Windows To Go certified. Whatever the case, you'll be informed and will need to remedy the situation before moving forward.

Some problems are a little more complex though. For instance, at least in our scenario where we're using the wizard to create a single drive, you might not be able to enable BitLocker during the creation process. This can be caused by restrictions that have been applied to your computer, set by Group Policy in an enterprise or with local policies on a local machine. These policies are located in the **Computer Configuration\Policies\ Administrative Templates\Windows Components\BitLocker Drive Encryption** folder of the Group Policy editor. See Figure 2-7.

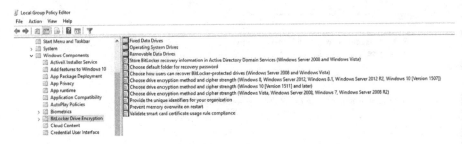

Figure 2-7. BitLocker Drive Encryption can be restricted in Group Policy

The reason why this happens is that the Windows To Go drive is considered a removable drive, and often policies are set to restrict what can be done with those types of drives by end users. Those restrictions can limit the use of BitLocker for you, too. Here are a few things to consider should you find yourself in this position:

> **Open the Removable Data Drives folder in Group Policy, shown in Figure 2-8, and check the setting for Control use of BitLocker on removable drives**. If this setting is disabled BitLocker cannot be applied to removable drives, and thus, the Windows To Go Creator wizard fails to add a BitLocker password at this point. Remove the restriction to resolve this problem.

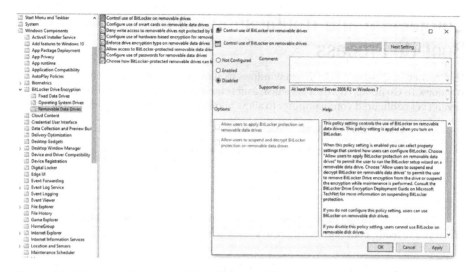

Figure 2-8. *Windows To Go is considered a removable drive, so any Group Policy settings applicable to these drives will apply here*

In the same **Removable Data Drives folder, check the setting for Configure use of smart cards on removable data drives**. If enabled along with the option to **Require use of smart cards on removable data drives, the** BitLocker configuration step might fail if you did not sign on with your smart card credentials before starting the Windows To Go Creator process.

In the same **folder, check the status for Configure use of passwords for removable data drives.** If this setting is enabled and the password is required to be complex, the computer must be able to contact the domain controller to verify that the password you've typed meets set requirements. If it can't access this controller, BitLocker drive encryption will not succeed.

Completing and Troubleshooting the Boot-Up Process

You learned in Chapter 1 how to use Windows to allow a computer to boot from a Windows To Go drive. There's a graphical user interface just for that purpose. If you haven't yet configured your computer to allow booting to Windows To Go, do that now:

1. Click Win+W or open a Search window.

2. Type "Change Windows To Go startup options" and click enter.

3. Select Yes.

4. Click Save Changes.

Make sure to also set the firmware to boot to USB first, also outlined in Chapter 1. When you're ready, continue on to boot to your Windows To Go workspace for the first time.

Booting Your Windows To Go Workspace

Now it's time to see how the new Windows To Go drive works. Follow these steps to boot to your Windows To Go workspace:

1. Wake up or turn on the host PC.

2. Insert the Windows To Go USB drive directly into a USB 3.0 or USB 2.0 port on the PC; it won't work if you plug it into a USB extender.

3. Turn on or restart the PC.

4. If your Windows To Go drive is protected with BitLocker, when prompted type the password.

When you boot your Windows To Go drive for the first time, it'll look like and act like you're booting to a brand-new operating system that's never been used. You'll be required to work through the normal setup process, just as you would with any new machine. The Windows To Go workspace will take inventory of the host machine and load any necessary drivers, and you'll be prompted to input a product ID, configure settings, and do all of the other necessary setup tasks required of any new Windows installation. Once that's done, it's done. You won't have to do it again. However, there might be a small delay when booting to a computer you've never booted to before, while the applicable drivers load. There will be more on setting up a new Windows To Go drive later in the section entitled Working With a New Installation of Windows To Go, later in this chapter.

Explore Common Boot Problems

Like anything, more than a few things can go wrong when trying to boot to a Windows To Go drive. Most of the time it's a problem with the firmware, which has not been configured to boot to a USB drive. Problems occur when the PC ignores the Windows To Go drive, for whatever reason. Other times it's a mismatch between the host and the drive. Refer to

Table 1-1 in Chapter 1 for compatibility information. However, sometimes the problem is more complex. On occasion you'll run across a drive that will boot but won't work properly because it isn't imaged with a genuine copy of Windows. However there are other things that can go awry. Here are few things to look at should you still have problems:

- Make sure the most up-to-date BIOS is installed.

- Verify the drive is inserted into the host and not into an external USB hub.

- If the drive won't boot while inserted into a host's USB 3.0 port, try a USB 2.0 port.

Explore Hardware Issues

If your troubleshooting techniques prove that the problem doesn't stem from a BIOS or port issue, perhaps you're trying to boot to an incompatible host like a Mac. Mac computers don't support Windows To Go. Additionally, you can't use Windows To Go on devices with ARM processors, such as those found in the older Windows RT machines. So, explore that next and verify the host is compatible and is of the right type and architecture.

Finally, you might see errors that state that Windows is "installing devices" even though devices were installed the last time you connected Windows To Go to a specific host. This sometimes happens when third-party drivers for different hardware use the same device IDs or service names, and when Windows To Go is used to roam among these devices. Problems occur when conflicts occur. This is a more complicated error and will require the services of a network administrator to straighten out, and it is beyond the scope of this chapter.

Explore Group Policy Boot Parameter Settings

You learned earlier that problems can occur when creating Windows To Go drives with regard to trying to enable BitLocker when Group Policy settings prohibit such configurations. Likewise, Group Policy can be used to allow or disallow booting to portable operating systems. If you are having boot issues and you think this is the case, from the host or from the domain controller as applicable, navigate to **Computer Configuration\Administrative Templates\Windows Components\Portable Operating System\Windows To Go Default Startup Options** and take a look at the settings. See Figure 2-9.

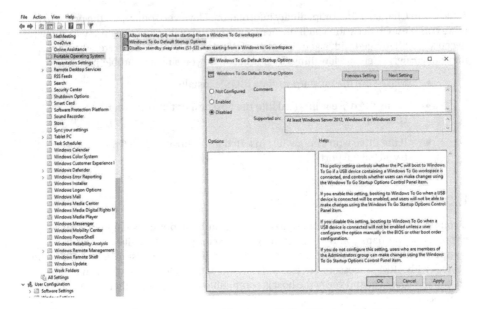

Figure 2-9. *If boot problems persist, consider Group Policy Windows To Go Startup Options settings*

If the policy is disabled, you need to enable this policy to let Windows look for a connected USB Windows To Go drive. Even when disabled though, note that a user can still configure the option to boot to USB in the firmware settings. If you do not configure this policy setting, Administrators can use the Windows To Go Startup Options to enable or disable booting from a USB drive, as outlined in Chapters 1 and 2.

Working with a New Installation of Windows To Go

The first time you boot to a new Windows To Go workspace you'll be prompted to work through the required setup tasks, just as you would with any new Windows installation. You'll want to be patient through this first experience, as it might take a little more time than you think it should for Windows to start, and the Windows To Go workspace might even reboot before the setup screen appears.

Setup tasks include but are not limited to the following:

- Setting your country, language, keyboard layout and time zone.

- Accepting the terms of volume licensing for Windows Enterprise editions or inputting a product ID for other versions.

- Choosing to use Express settings or configuring setting manually.

- Connecting to a wireless network (Ethernet will be automatically connected)

- Waiting while updates are applied.

- Choosing how you'll connect, perhaps joining an Azure AD or a domain, or none.

- Creating an account and entering a password and password hint.

Once it's set up, the Desktop will appear. Figure 2-10 shows a Windows 10 Windows To Go Desktop. If you open File Explorer you won't see the host's hard drive, although you will see shared resources if you opt to set your network to Private when prompted, if you join a home group, or if you turn on File and Printer Sharing manually.

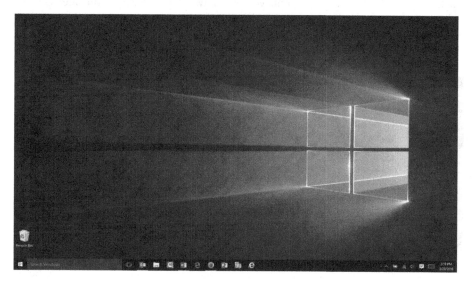

Figure 2-10. *A Windows To Go desktop looks exactly like a regular Windows desktop*

Now, find out if Windows has been activated. You can do that from any compatible computer, but on a Windows 10 machine you do it by clicking Start and then Settings. Click Update and Security, and then Activation. If necessary, work through the process to activate your new workspace.

WINDOWS TO GO WORKSPACES CAN'T BE ACCESSED BY THE HOST PC

By default, when Windows To Go workspaces are created, drive letters are not automatically assigned to the new workspace. That's why you can't see the Windows To Go drive when it's plugged into a running computer. However, if you really need to access the files on the Windows To Go drive from a host, you can use diskmgmt.msc or DiskPart to assign a drive letter to the workspace.

Accessing Personal and Local Resources

You can access some local resources when logged into a Windows To Go workspace, and there are ways to access your personal files. However, when you're logged in to a Windows To Go workspace, it as if you are working only from that operating system and appears as though no host is involved. Thus, you can't access files and folders that are stored on the host, and you can't access the host's hard drive.

Here's an example. Take a look at Figure 2-11. Notice that you can only see Local Disk (C:) and the host's DVD drive. You can't access or see the host's hard disk. You can access some local resources though. For instance, you can see and use the host's DVD drive. You can install software from that drive onto your Windows To Go workspace, provided Group Policies don't prevent it. You can access printers and other resources that are connected to a network you've joined and have appropriate permissions for, perhaps those available in a home group or those made public on the local network.

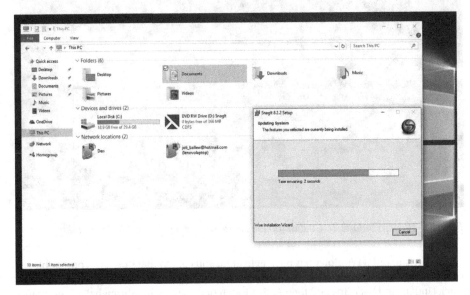

Figure 2-11. *Use the host's DVD drive to install hardware onto the Windows To Go drive*

With regard to personal files and folders, there are several ways to work and to store data using a portable workspace. Users can store data to a SharePoint site, for instance, or to a third-party online solution, like Dropbox. Corporations might put something else into effect like DirectAccess. You'll learn about this in Chapter 3.

For small business or home users, roaming technicians, or independent contractors (among other things), something simpler might be in order. One solution is to use OneDrive. It's easy to log on to OneDrive from the Windows To Go workspace, and is the solution I use most often (as an independent contractor). Avoid saving data to the Windows To Go workspace though; if the drive is lost, so is your data.

To sign in to OneDrive from Windows To Go configured with a Windows 10 image:

1. Click Start and click Settings.

2. Click Accounts.

3. Click Your email and accounts (or just Accounts).

4. Click Sign in With a Microsoft Account Instead. See Figure 2-12.

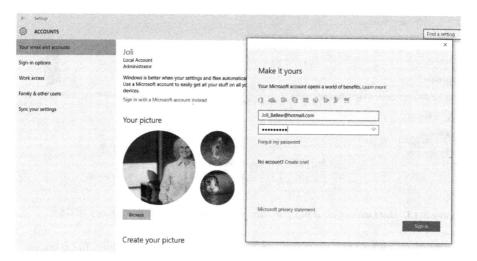

Figure 2-12. *Opt to log in with a Microsoft Account to gain access to OneDrive*

5. Input your user name and password and click Sign In.

6. If prompted to complete additional tasks, such as receiving and inputting a confirmation code, do so.

7. Set a PIN (personal identification number) if desired, when prompted, or opt to skip this step.

8. Open File Explorer by clicking the folder icon on the Taskbar

9. Click OneDrive

10. If you have files saved there already, you'll have access to them, as shown in figure 2-13.

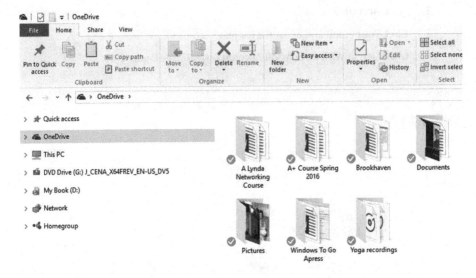

Figure 2-13. OneDrive offers a place to save your work while using Windows To Go

To sign in with a Microsoft Account from a Windows 8-based Windows To Go image:

1. Swipe in from the right edge of the screen, tap Settings, and then tap Change PC settings.
   (If you're using a mouse, point to the lower-right corner of the screen, move the mouse pointer up, click Settings, and then click Change PC settings.)

2. Tap or click Accounts, and then tap or click Your account.

3. Click Connect to a Microsoft Account.

4. Select the desired option. You will need to choose among these:

   a. Connect to an existing Microsoft Account

   b. Sign up with the e-mail address you use most often

   c. Get a new e-mail address

5. Work through the resulting prompts to complete the process.

■ **Caution**   It isn't a good idea (or a Best Practice) to save files to the Windows To Go workspace. If the USB drive is lost, so is the data. Save instead to OneDrive or something similar, using folder redirection, or another, similar, enterprise solution.

Note that other local resources might exist, like printers or scanners. Figure 2-14 shows two things. The first is a locally attached printer. This particular printer is attached to the host that the Windows To Go drive has booted with. The Windows To Go user can print to that printer. The second is a printer on the local area network attached to another computer. This is available via the Web and is accessible because, in this instance, the Windows To Go workspace has been enabled to use File and Printer Sharing and has been joined the local home group. This won't always be the case of course, but do note that some local resources will be available to your end users.

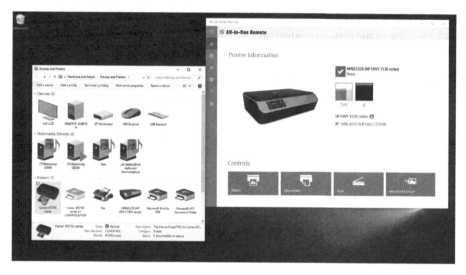

Figure 2-14. *Some local resources are available to Windows To Go users, like printers directly attached to hosts and wireless or Internet printers*

■ **Note**   When you sign into your Microsoft Account, even on a Windows To Go drive, language settings, keyboard preferences, wallpaper, themes and various other settings will be applied. Once this happens, you'll feel a sense of familiarity, and once you set up all of you applications you might find it hard to tell if you're working on a real host or a USB stick.

Accessing Domain Resources

In the previous section I talked about how to access local resources while using a Windows To Go drive on a host, on a local area network. I enabled File and Printer sharing, and I joined the available home group to get to all of these resources. Local networks are a lot different from domains though. When you use Windows To Go with domain credentials, a different set of things occurs.

Before continuing here, if you are in a position to join a domain by connecting to a domain server, you can do so by following these steps. Note that these are instructions for a Windows 10 Windows To Go workspace:

1. Click Start and click Settings.

2. Click System.

3. Click About.

4. Click Join a Domain.

5. Input the domain credentials. See Figure 2-15.

Figure 2-15. *If you need to join a domain, do so from the System window*

Much of the time though this isn't how joining a domain works for the end user. The Windows To Go workspace is generally already set and users connect to the domain using the same tools they'd use from a laptop or other mobile devices. There are likely even shortcuts on the Desktop to facilitate these connections, so that there is similarity and familiarity to lessen support calls and technical issues, especially if VPNs are involved.

Beyond leaving users to their own devices (so to speak), there are other ways to manage domain users and give them access to domain resources. One is Offline Domain Join. This feature lets administrators join workspaces to the domain without the devices being connected to the company intranet. This is one way to enable access. However, with users connecting from so many different devices, other options might be used instead.

One other option is to use DirectAccess. The intranet will have to be configured to support it, but once in place DirectAccess provides easy access to resources on the company domain. When users log on to the workspace using their domain credentials, they can access the domain resources as if they were directly connected to the intranet.

Best Practices for End Users

It's important to educate users as well as network administrators on Microsoft's Best Practices list for Windows To Go. This list summarizes the most important things to keep in mind:

- Always shut down Windows To Go like you would any machine.

- Wait for Windows To Go to completely shut down before removing the drive.

- Although you can, it's best not to insert the Windows To Go drive into a running computer. Turn off the computer, insert the drive, and turn the computer back on.

- Plug the Windows To Go drive directly into a USB port. Don't use a USB hub.

- If you can, use a USB 3.0 port with Windows To Go. If that doesn't work, use USB 2.0.

- Avoid installing non-Microsoft core USB drivers onto a Windows To Go workspace.

- In a large environment, select and use a standard USB drive that is certified for Windows To Go and deploy it across the organization. Consistency is the key to management happiness.

- Plan how users can use Windows To Go, and set Group Policies appropriately.

- Offer information on how to enable booting on host computers, and educate your IT department or help desk on how to help users who have problems with the boot process.

Troubleshooting Additional End-User Experience Issues

Your end users will likely have issues that haven't been addressed here, and while there is no way to address everything, there are a few common questions users ask and mistakes they make that can cause problems. One of the most common is when the user makes a habit of removing the Windows To Go drive while the operating system is running. When

31

this happens the host computer could stall or freeze. In this case, and if the user reinserts the drive within a minute of removing it, it should pick up where it left off. If not, or if the user inserts the drive into a different port on the host, problems will likely ensue. It might be that the host computer turns itself off, or the Windows To Go drive becomes corrupt.

Users might also run into issues where they want Windows To Go to hibernate or go to sleep, and they express concerns about why it does not. Windows To Go doesn't support hibernation by default. Although network administrators can change this default behavior through Group Policy settings, they often do not, because when a Windows To Go workspace hibernates, it will only resume successfully on the exact same hardware. Since this likely won't happen, and because the user state will be lost during the transition, hibernation is disabled.

If you are positive that you will use a specific Windows To Go drive on the same computer it uses to hibernate with, you can enable hibernation using the Windows To Go Group Policy setting, Allow hibernate (S4) when started from a Windows To Go workspace that is located at **Computer Configuration\Administrative Templates\Windows Components\Portable Operating System** in the Local Group Policy Editor (gpedit.msc)

Another problem users run into is with applications installed on a Windows To Go drive. Although installed applications should work most of the time, issues arise on occasion. If an application uses a specific hardware binding for licensing reasons (or digital rights) those applications might not run on different hardware. In this case the user will only be able to run the applications on the same host on which it was first installed.

Finally, and along those same lines, for Windows 8 users, note that Windows Store apps use a similar hardware binding for managing licenses. When a user tries to run store apps on more than one machine, problems ensue. That's why the Windows Store is disabled by default in Windows To Go on Windows 8. If it were enabled there would be licensing issues when using apps purchased in the Store. With Windows 8.1 and up though, the licensing used by the Windows Store has been updated. These problems have been resolved.

Summary

Getting a Windows To Go drive up and running and using it to experiment while learning is an excellent place to start your Windows To Go studies. You did that in this chapter. Learning how the system boots and what to expect is also important. You certainly need to know what your end users will experience and what problems they might encounter. In the rest of the chapters we'll look at Windows To Go from an administrator's point of view, starting with Chapter 3, where we begin to prepare the enterprise for Windows To Go.

CHAPTER 3

■ ■ ■

Prepare Your Small Business, School, or Enterprise for Windows To Go

You learned in the last two chapters that the Windows To Go Creator is available in Windows 8-based and Windows 10 Enterprise editions and that Windows To Go USB drives are generally provisioned in larger enterprises. Those drives are offered to mobile employees to provide an operating system when a laptop or tablet isn't available. Small businesses also use Windows To Go, though, as do educational institutions. As long as an Enterprise edition is available, a solution is available.

In this chapter I'll touch on three scenarios (business, education, and enterprise), and what kinds of things must be considered before any Windows To Go solution is put into place. Before we start though, note that when I mention small business, I'm thinking along the lines of a company that has fewer than 20 or so computers. There are midsized businesses too, perhaps up to 500, and enterprise businesses have more than that, and can range up to the thousands. If you're still wondering if Windows To Go will suit your specific needs though in whatever scenario you have, let's recap some ways Windows To Go can be used before we get started.

■ **Note** Even if you are planning to use Windows To Go in an enterprise, I suggest reading the entire chapter anyway, even the parts aimed at small businesses or single users. Create a few drives, configure Folder Redirection, and see what it's like to use the drives too.

Possible scenarios you might run across include enabling users to work at home while also maintaining a corporate desktop experience. This is a common one. You might also want to enable sole proprietors or small business contractors to work away from the office without having to worry about carrying a laptop or tablet, or to enable all users to travel lightly when they are headed somewhere a host computer is available to them on a temporary basis, and where the work is short term, perhaps as little as an hour or a single afternoon.

© Joli Ballew 2016
J. Ballew, *Windows To Go*, DOI 10.1007/978-1-4842-2134-1_3

With regard to education, teachers can use Windows To Go to provide a workstation that students can use both at school and at home, provided they can find a computer they can use to boot with. Students can save their work to a cloud drive, and whatever laptops are available for students can be used sparingly and only for those students for whom Windows To Go won't work.

■ **Note** Although Windows To Go isn't meant to replace desktops or mobile devices, it can provide a short-term solution to unique problems that enterprises encounter with users who roam from computer to computer or travel from job site to job site.

In this chapter you'll learn how to get started with Windows To Go in various scenarios. You'll inventory your current enterprise infrastructure, as applicable to your situation, to see if you have everything you need. When appropriate, you'll learn how to put necessary measures in place to make these technologies work, such as redirecting a folder on a Windows To Go workspace to a cloud drive and configuring Folder Redirection on a server. You'll learn how to configure Group Policy in specific scenarios and explore various ways to enable users to save data and user profiles. You'll also learn a little about DirectAccess in an enterprise.

It's important to note, also, before we get too far into this, that Windows Enterprise editions are only available through Volume Activation licensing. You'll learn about this in the next chapter. You can get personal copies of Windows Enterprise if you have a Microsoft Developer Network account (MSDN) though, but these aren't copies that are valid in a workplace. However, if you have an MSDN account and would like to follow along here, or if you're only going to use the software for personal use, you can get a copy of it for testing.

Verify Your Domain Enterprise Infrastructure Is Ready

There are three scenarios I'll cover in this chapter, Windows To Go in an enterprise, Windows To Go for small businesses, and Windows To Go for educational purposes. This part of the chapter deals with preparing your enterprise for Windows To Go, or perhaps more specifically, verifying that your enterprise is ready. Note that this is an extremely high-level overview; if you plan to deploy Windows To Go in an enterprise you'll need to read a lot more about Windows To Go than this and there will be a lot of planning and testing involved before you can actually implement a solution.

If your company already has a system in place to create, modify, manage, and deploy operating system images to desktop computers, you likely have all you need to create and provision Windows To Go workspaces. That's a lot easier said than done though. Quite a bit goes into making that possible, including planning, resources, manpower, software, and physical hardware, among other things. If your infrastructure already has a system in place to enable remote access to corporate resources, note that Windows To Go also works well and is compatible with those technologies. Windows To Go works well with

DirectAccess, folder redirection, and Remote Desktop, among other things. You'll learn a little more about that in this chapter, and I'll explore a few of these technologies.

Although all of these items are compatible and can function well with Windows To Go workspaces there are a few changes you might want to make, and I'll address that here too. Many enterprises create a separate image for the Windows To Go workspaces, images that are unique to the enterprise and specific to Windows To Go. Some create special groups of users and make appropriate changes to Group Policy for those groups as well. Do note though that if the infrastructure is already set for Windows To Go, these are minor issues. Let's take a look first at what you'll need to create your own images and deploy them as Windows To Go workspaces.

Infrastructure for Deploying Custom Windows Images

If you are a large enterprise and want to, or need to, create a Windows operating system that is unique to your environment, you can do that by creating custom Windows images. You certainly would not want to do this if you are a small business. It would take a lot less time to manually make changes to each computer in your workgroup than it would to set up a system that would enable you to do that.

There's a lot that has to be put in place to create a custom Windows image though, such as one you might want to put on a Windows To Go drive, and what you'll need to have it all configured before you can start. I'm not going to walk you through any specific deployment tasks in this section, such as how to set a specific server up to provide this functionality, that's not the scope of this chapter, but I do want to mention the tools you'll need to look into.

Since Windows 10 is the latest available operating system available, for the most part I'll address Windows 10 in this chapter and beyond. However, you can create images with Windows 7 or 8, or others, to meet whatever your needs are. In that vein then, one of the first things you'll want to do if you're going to deploy Windows 10 on to Windows To Go drives and you're going to want to be able to also manage upgrades beyond that, is to have a look at the Assessment and Deployment Toolkit (ADK). There is a new release to support Windows 10. Of course, there's an older release for Windows 8 and 8.1. In this chapter, though, and throughout the book I'll focus on what's required to perform these tasks with Windows 10. Thus, make sure you understand that you'll need the newer ADK for Windows 10 if that's what you want to deploy. It's backward compatible though; you can also use it to deploy Windows 7, Windows 8, and Windows 8.1. Figure 3-1 shows the installation options. For good measure I'll check all of them. You should too, if you're new to ADK.

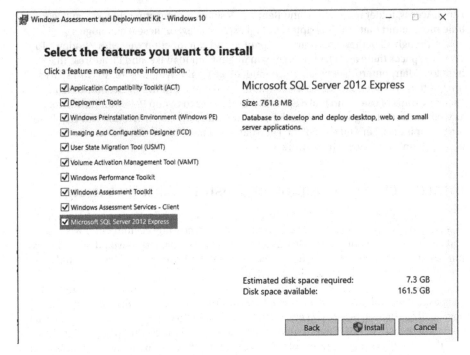

Figure 3-1. Install the Windows ADK for Windows 10

Windows ADK has existed for quite a while, as you likely know. However, improvements have been made to previous versions. Here's a short list of the improvements you'll find in this version of Windows ADK compared to older versions:

- New runtime provisioning capabilities

- Contains the Windows Imaging and Configuration Designer (Windows ICD)

- Incorporates updates for Deployment Image Servicing and Management (DISM)

- Includes updates for the User State Migration Tool (USMT)

- Includes updates for Windows Preinstallation Environment (Windows PE)

■ **Note**   You'll read a lot here about what needs to be upgraded and updated to support Windows 10. However, for mobile devices that you manage with Windows Intune (and other technologies) what was supported by Windows 8.1 is still fully supported in Windows 10. Keep in mind though that the new Windows 10 Mobile Device Management (MDM) settings will require updates to the MDM services.

You'll need more than this though to get started, if you're starting from scratch. You'll need the Microsoft Deployment Toolkit 2013 Update 1, available from Microsoft. For this software and others, simply search for what you want, and browse to it from the results. As with the ADK, this has also been updated to support Windows 10, and again, note that older versions have not.

System Center Configuration Manager has also been updated for Windows 10 support for both management and deployment. For more information about System Center Configuration Manager support for Windows 10, search at www.Microsoft.com for Deploy Windows 10 with System Center 2012 R2 Configuration Manager.

The Microsoft Desktop Optimization Pack (MDOP) has also been updated to support Windows 10. To support specific aspects of management and deployment consider these minimum requirements, shown in Table 3-1.

Table 3-1. *Product and Required Versions*

Product	Required version
Advanced Group Policy Management (AGPM)	AGPM 4.0 Service Pack 3
Application Virtualization (App-V)	App-V 5.1
Diagnostics and Recovery Toolkit (DaRT)	DaRT 10
Microsoft BitLocker Administration and Monitoring (MBAM)	MBAM 2.5 or 2.5 SP1
UE-V	UE-V 2.1 SP1

You'll also need to update Windows Server Update Services (WSUS). If you need to update your server, here's how to do it:

1. Select Options, and then click Products and Classifications. See Figure 3-2.

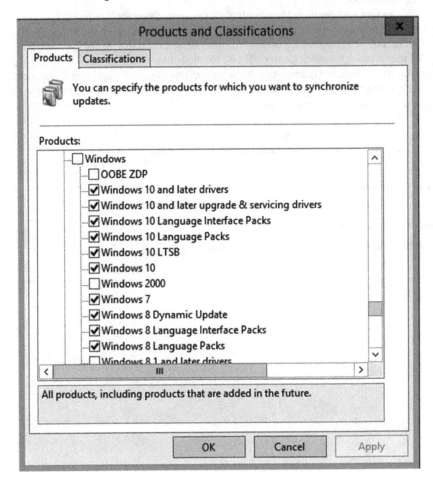

Figure 3-2. Select the desired products

2. Expand the Products tree, and select at least Windows 10 and Windows 10 LTSB products. You can select others.

3. Click OK.

4. Expand the Synchronizations node, right-click, and choose Synchronize Now.

There are other items you need to consider, and I suggest you do a lot of reading before you continue in your enterprise. However, I believe that if you are in a position to need custom Windows To Go images, you are also in a position to create them, once you update your current infrastructure to support it.

Verify your Small Business or Educational Setting Is Ready

If you have a small business that consists of a workgroup of say, fewer than 20 or 30 computers, work in a small private school, or are a sole proprietor and use a workgroup or peer-to-peer network to share resources, all you really need to get started is a copy of Windows Enterprise and a few Windows To Go-compatible USB drives. You can use the Windows To Go Creator to create the workspaces and use an unaltered image of whatever Windows version you want to use. There's no need to try to create a custom image just for a few people. Consider if you want to deploy Windows 7 or Windows 8.1 workspaces, though, perhaps making that choice if you or your users are more comfortable with the older technology, but note that it's certainly possible to create those workspaces with Windows 10.

Once the drives are created, and note that you'll need a valid product ID for each, you and your employees can use the drives to do work. You'll want to put some sort of solution in practice for users to save the data they create while using those drives though, so make sure to read the next few sections that have to do with folder redirection and offline files. You do not want users saving data to those USB workspaces. If the drive is lost, so is the data. Also, make sure to enable BitLocker on all of the drives as outlined in Chapter 2.

Consider Folder Redirection, Offline Files, and UE-V

After you've met your infrastructure requirements, you need to consider how you are going to manage users and their data once you have the drives in place and users utilizing their Windows To Go drive. You can't very well have users save data to their USB stick. You'll need to make sure they are saving their data to a safe place each and every time. This can be difficult if users share a single computer, but it's not that difficult to do for a Windows To Go drive. It's also imperative that they have access to their data and personal user profiles from wherever they are too, so they'll need some way to access the domain and enterprise resources.

■ **Note** A User Profile is a collection of settings that includes desktop backgrounds, screensavers, mouse preferences, sound settings, and other features. The general population, like users in home or small business settings, manages their own profiles. In an enterprise, the user profile settings can be managed by group policies.

Folder Redirection for a Single Workspace and User

There are a few options available to you, as a network administrator, to manage user data. One of the most important things is to make sure that users don't save data to their USB drives. That data would be lost if the drive were lost. Data must be stored elsewhere. To do that you configure Folder Redirection. This feature lets you forward the data users save to a network location on your domain servers, a SharePoint site, or even a public site like OneDrive or GoogleDrive. On an end user's workspace, folder redirection is achieved from the Properties tab of the folder you want to redirect.

In this example I'll redirect a folder for a Windows 10 workspace to OneDrive. Folder redirection hasn't changed much so if you are using Windows 8 or 8.1 the directions are basically the same. If you're following along at home, say, are part of a small business, and don't have a domain to work with, you can perform these steps to get an idea of what folder redirection is like:

1. Open File Explorer.

2. Locate the Documents folder or other folder to redirect.

3. Right-click the folder and click Properties.

4. Click the Location tab. See Figure 3-3.

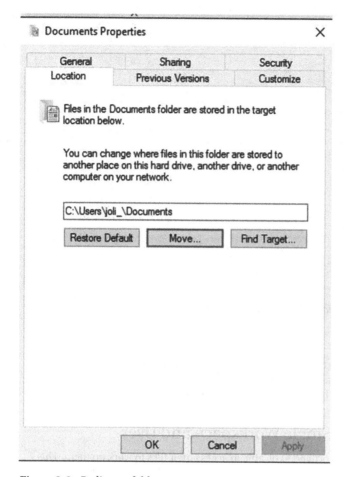

Figure 3-3. *Redirect a folder*

5. Click Move.

6. Browse to the location of the drive to save to.

7. Click Select Folder as shown in Figure 3-4.

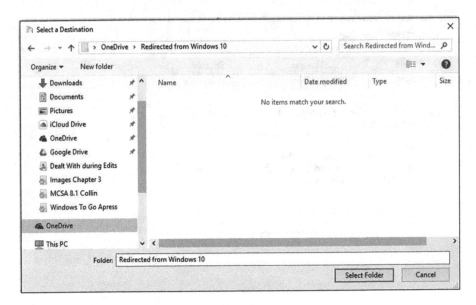

Figure 3-4. *Select the desired folder to redirect data to*

8. Click OK.

Now, any data saved to the Documents folder for this user will be saved to the OneDrive folder instead. Users won't notice any difference though, and there's nothing to teach them to do to make it happen. Folder redirection is seamless to the user.

Offline Files for a Single Workspace and User

With folder redirection, users need to be able to access their files to work on them. This can be achieved through any Internet connection. But when users don't save files to an Internet server like Google Drive or OneDrive, and instead save their files to a local network share, things get a little more complicated.

So one of the main problems that needs to be addressed with users working remotely on Windows To Go drives is that users won't be able to access the personal files stored on network shares from just anywhere. If the files they need to access are stored, say, on a computer at their office, and there's no domain or other solution in place to access that desktop computer remotely, they are simply out of luck. With offline files, users can access their personal data even when they aren't connected to the network where the data resides. That's because files are copied to the drive and are available to them when needed. This has several advantages:

- Copies of important files are saved to the Windows To Go workspace, so they are available even when users can't access their files via a network.

- Even if users have a way to access their files from a network share, if there's no Internet connection and there is need for it, those files are still available to users from their drives.

- Users are not affected when a local network "goes down." Users can continue to work without interruption.

- It's easy to sync files once a network becomes available. Users simply need to click the Sync button if they are using Sync Center to perform this task.

- It's possible to work with offline files when a network is slow and cumbersome.

Enable Offline Files and Folders

Before you can configure and use Offline Files you need to enable Offline Files. Here's how to do that in Windows 10, and as noted before, performing these steps in other operating system versions is similar:

1. Open Control Panel and, if applicable, click Category under View by and click Large icons. See Figure 3-5.

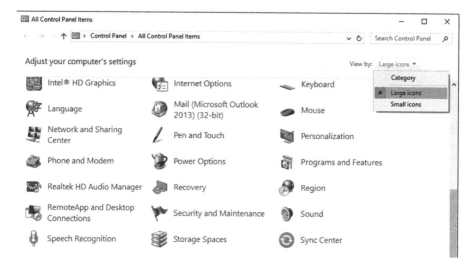

Figure 3-5. *Open Sync Center*

2. Click Sync Center.

3. Click Manage offline files.

4.   Click Enable offline files. See Figure 3-6.

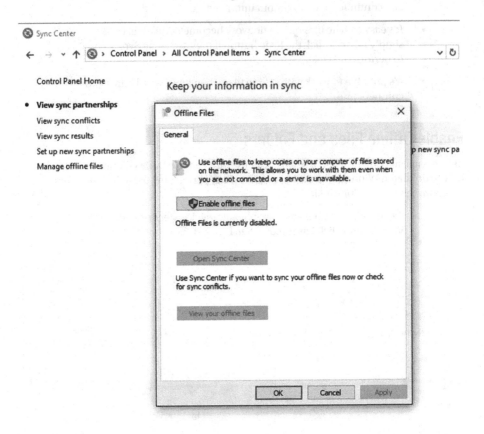

Figure 3-6. Enable offline files

5.   Click OK.

6.   Save any open work and restart the computer.

Once you've enabled this feature you're ready to configure the files you want to make available offline. So now, connect to the local network that contains the files you want to copy, and locate the network resource. If you're setting up offline files in a workgroup:

1.   Open File Explorer.

2.   Expand Network. See Figure 3-7.

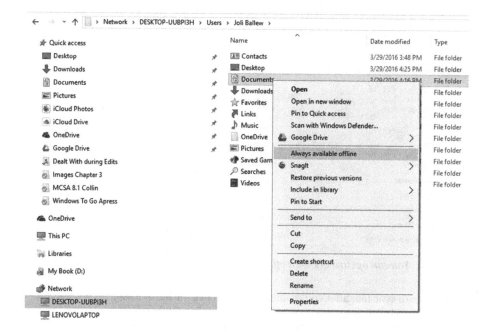

Figure 3-7. *Choose the folders to configure as offline files*

3. Navigate to the applicable folder.

4. Right-click the folder and click Always available offline.

5. Wait while the process completes.

Manage Offline Files and Folders

Users might be concerned about how offline files work or what they need to do to make sure that there are no problems with versioning when working offline. You can assure your users that they'll work with offline files just as they would any file. They navigate to it, open the file, do their work, and then save the changes. It's possible to work offline even if you are connected to a network too, though, perhaps because the connection is slow or you know you're going to encounter network issues while working.

To opt to work offline even if you are online in a Windows 10 workspace, keep in mind that this feature has been available for years and performing these steps with other operating system versions is similar:

1. Navigate to the file or folder.

2. Click it one time to select it.

3. From the toolbar under the Home tab, click Easy access.

4. Click Work Offline. (If it says Work Online, you're already working offline). See Figure 3-8.

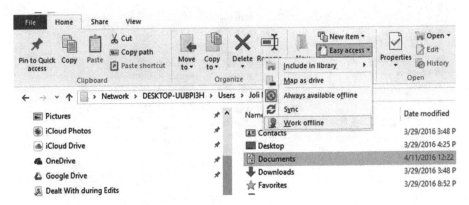

Figure 3-8. You can opt to work with offline files even if you are connected to a network

5. To sync files after you're finished, right-click the file or folder and click Sync, then Sync selected offline files. (If there's a conflict, you'll be informed. More on this later.)

If you want to see all of your offline files, review their status, and see if there are any sync conflicts, open Sync Center. From here you can:

- Browse to synced files

- Sync all files

- View and set up new sync partnerships

- View conflicts (older and newer versions of files)

- Manage synced files

WHAT HAPPENS WHEN THERE IS A SYNC CONFLICT?

When you opt to enable offline files and folders and choose a folder to sync, a copy of that data is stored on your computer. You can work on those files there, and when you reconnect to the network, Windows starts the sync process automatically. When working online, sync is seamless. When working offline, Windows syncs when you reconnect. If you've made changes to the file on your computer and someone else has made changes to the original on the network drive Windows detects that conflict and prompts you regarding how you'd like to handle the situation. You can opt to create a second copy, or you can choose which of the two versions you'd like to keep.

Consider UE-V with Folder Redirection for Educational Institutions or Small Businesses

UE-V (User Experience Virtualization) technology lets users access their user profile from virtually anywhere. As noted earlier, a user profile holds the settings that a user configures on a computer, such as a screensaver, desktop background, and sound schemes, among other things.

Generally the user profile is stored on a user's computer, such as a desktop or laptop. When Windows To Go is used independently of other solutions, the profile is stored on the USB drive. A user profile can also be stored in OneDrive, so that when a user logs on with his or her Microsoft account, the user profile is loaded.

UE-V with Folder Redirection and Offline Files is a common solution for all kinds of scenarios, though, and proves quite valuable for the end users as well as for the network administrators. In fact, it is the recommended method for providing access to data and settings with Windows To Go, because it delivers the best combination of flexibility and manageability for practically any infrastructure.

With UE-V, Folder Redirection, and Offline Files in place, your employees will always have a desktop they recognize, no matter where they log on. The consistency helps users feel comfortable right away, because the Windows To Go experience can be tailored to suit their needs. If they do have a desktop at work, the workspace can be configured to mimic that look too.

These three components are summarized here, as it relates to the network infrastructure:

- UE-V can be used to synchronize users' settings with a network file share. Changes made to Windows To Go settings while a user roams are synced with the file share when it becomes available.

- UE-V can sync application settings. Like users' settings, changes made to application settings are synchronized with the file share when that share becomes available.

- Folder Redirection uses a file share too. Data is stored on the file share so that the user can access the data no matter where they log on.

- Offline Files copies configured files and folders to the Windows To Go workspace so that they are accessible even if the device isn't connected to the network. Configuring Offline Files is essential if users are required to take their Windows To Go workspaces home with them, or are expected to work while using the Windows To Go drive.

- All of this works together. UE-V settings, application settings, and data are all stored to applicable redirected folders.

Of course, Windows To Go workspaces can be configured to redirect these settings and data to the cloud instead of network shares. OneDrive and Office 365 are just two solutions. Anyone can get OneDrive storage, so OneDrive is a viable solution for sole proprietors and small businesses. Users only need a Microsoft account to get started.

OneDrive can be used to store:

- Data.
- Internet Explorer favorites.
- Desktop settings.
- Application settings.

Office 365 is another option. Office 365 offers cloud storage as well as a full version of Microsoft Office. While this solution can work for larger enterprises, it's important to note that Office 365 offers educational institution plans for schools and institutions. Beyond that, there are free plans for students and faculty. While the options offered so far are common solutions, note that other solutions are available. SharePoint, GoogleDrive, and DropBox are just a few.

Table 3-2 sums up what we've talked about so far, and details the options for data and settings storage.

Table 3-2. Summary of Data and Storage Options

Store in WTG Workspace	Folder Redirection with UE-V	OneDrive
Requires no additional configuration	Requires network and Group Policy infrastructure	User must log on with a Microsoft account
No expertise needed	Requires Information Technology (IT) Professional	No expertise needed
Loss of drive means loss of data	Backup method in place by network administrator	Cloud based and backed up in data center
No roaming capabilities	User can roam	Roaming enabled as long as user logs in with a Microsoft account
Requires no bandwidth or Internet connection	Requires intranet access	Requires Internet access

Folder Redirection and Offline Files for Network Administrators

So far I've introduced options for saving data off the Windows To Go drive for small businesses and sole proprietors. If you are a network administrator in a larger enterprise and you are interested in setting up folder redirection and offline files for your domain, that's a different setup, and you have a lot of work to do before you can make that happen. While I can't walk you through that entire process, I can guide you through the steps you'll need to take to put the process into place.

Before we start, note that you'll need to have administrator privileges. You can be a member of the Domain Administrators security group, the Enterprise Administrators security group, or the Group Policy Creator Owners security group. Client computers can run just about anything, including Windows 10, Windows 8.1, Windows 8, Windows 7,

Windows Vista, and Windows XP. If you're interested in using servers, Windows Server 2012 R2, Windows Server 2012, Windows Server 2008 R2, Windows Server 2008, or Windows Server 2003 are compatible.

All of the computers you want to manage need to be part of an Active Directory domain. Although it seems obvious perhaps, you'll need to have a file server to start. That file server will hold the data for the folders you want to redirect.

■ **Note** Folder Redirection and Offline Files are not available for Windows RT.

Step 1: Create a Folder Redirection Security Group

You must create a group that contains users you want to apply folder redirection policy settings for. The way you do that varies depending on the Microsoft server version you are running. Because of this, these are fairly generic steps here to get you started, but I wanted to offer something to guide you through the process. So, if you don't already have this process in place, here are some basic guidelines:

1. Open Server Manager. It must have Active Directory Administration Center installed.

2. Click Tools, and click Active Directory Administration Center.

3. Right-click the domain or OU (organizational unit), click New, and then opt to create a new group.

4. Type a name for the group and make it a global group.

5. Select the appropriate entities to add to the group.

6. Type the names of the users or groups to which you want to deploy.

7. Complete the process as applicable.

Step 2: Create a File Share for Redirected Folders

You need a file share on a server running Windows Server 2012. To create this share, and as was mentioned before these are fairly generic steps:

1. Click File and Storage Services from the Server Manager Navigation pane.

2. Click Shares.

3. Click Tasks.

4. Click New Share.

5. Using the wizard to complete the process:

    a. Click SMB Share - Quick if you have File Server Resource
        Manager installed.

    b. Click SMB-Share Advanced if you do not.

    c. Select the server where you want to create the share.

    d. Name the share. (You can put a $ after the name to hide
        the share.)

    e. Clear the Enable continuous availability checkbox,
        if applicable. If desired, select Enable access-based
        enumeration and Encrypt data access.

6. Click Customize Permissions.

7. Click Disable inheritance. Click Convert inherited
    permissions into explicit permission on this object.

8. Set the permissions as follows, see Figure 3-9:

    a. SYSTEM – Full control for folders, subfolders, and files

    b. Administrators – Full control for this folder only

    c. CREATOR OWNER – Full control for subfolders and files

    d. Folder Redirection Users – List Folder/Read Data, Create
        Folders/Append Data this folder only

    e. Other groups – no permissions

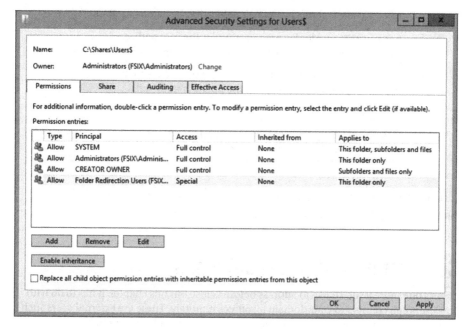

Figure 3-9. *Set security permissions*

9. Complete the wizard by setting the User Files folder usage value or the quota value, as applicable.

10. Click Create.

Step 3: Create a GPO for Folder Redirection

If you do not already have a Group Policy Object (GPO) created for Folder Redirection settings, you'll need to create one. You do this in Server Manager, from Tools, and Group Policy Management. You'll create a new GPO, set the scope, and add the new security group.

Step 4: Configure and Enable Folder Redirection with Offline Files

Now, you'll configure Group Policy. Here's how:

1. In Group Policy Management, right-click the GPO you just created.

2. Expand User Configuration, Policies, Windows Settings, and Folder Redirection.

3. Right-click the folder to redirect and click Properties.

4. Click Basic – Redirect Everyone's Folder To The Same Location.

5. Click Create a folder for each user under the root path, and then in the Root Path box type the path to the file share.

6. From the Settings tab, click Redirect the folder back to the local user profile location when the policy is removed.

7. Click OK and then Yes.

8. Now, from Group Policy Management, right-click the GPO you created and click Link Enabled.

■ **Note** Have users log on regularly to their Windows To Go drives to keep Active Directory (AD) computer account objects from becoming stale.

Considerations for DirectAccess

There's one more issue I'd like to address before I close out this chapter. It has to do with how users can connect to your domain resources remotely. These are external users such as contractors or corporate users who need to access your network remotely.

We've talked about what has to be put into place with regard to storing data on domain servers, but how will users connect, exactly? One way is to use Windows 2012 DirectAccess. With DirectAccess, client computers are always connected to your organization. You don't have to worry about users initiating connections or closing connections, or even about connectivity problems. Additionally, IT administrators can manage DirectAccess client computers whenever they are running and connected to the Internet.

The following server operating systems support DirectAccess. You can deploy:

-   all versions of Windows Server® 2008 R2 as a DirectAccess client or a DirectAccess server.

-   all versions of Windows Server® 2012 R2 as a DirectAccess client or a DirectAccess server.

-   all versions of Windows Server® 2012 as a DirectAccess client or a DirectAccess server.

The following client operating systems support DirectAccess.

-   Windows 10® Enterprise

-   Windows 10® Enterprise 2015 Long Term Servicing Branch (LTSB)

-   Windows® 8 Enterprise

-   Windows® 7 Ultimate

-   Windows® 7 Enterprise

Summary

In this chapter you learned how to inventory your current enterprise network infrastructure to see how you can best utilize Windows To Go now, and what upgrades you'll need to put into effect to provision Windows To Go drives if you want to do so with Windows 10. If you own a home or small business you learned how to use Windows To Go to roam effectively, exploring various storage options for users and their user profiles and data. In Chapter 4 you'll learn about activation and volume licensing.

CHAPTER 4

■ ■ ■

Understand Single Activations, Volume Licensing, and Software Assurance

Before you finalize a plan to create and provision Windows To Go drives in your enterprise, small business, or educational setting, you need to put a plan into place to activate them. There are several options, and you'll want to compare those options to find out which one works best for you. Note that if you already have a volume license, you can use what you have in place. This chapter is for those who do not yet have an activation solution.

Activate a Single Windows To Go Workspace

The simplest activation option is the one that applies to single drives created for personal use. You have a copy of Windows Enterprise, you've purchased a compatible Windows To Go drive and you've installed an operating system on it using the Windows To Go Creator. These types of Windows To Go workspaces require an activation key just like any copy of Windows would. To input this key, boot to the Windows To Go drive, walk through the setup process just as you would with any Windows installation, and when prompted input the applicable product key. You'll be required to activate the operating system too, once it's up and running, just as you would with any OS.

You will see the prompt to activate in various ways, depending on the operating system installed. For instance, in Windows 8 and 8.1 you could be prompted when you open the Settings charm and try to make configuration changes. You might simply see a prompt that pops up in the bottom right corner of the screen, near the notification area. You can also navigate to the activation area manually. In Windows 8 or 8.1, go to the Start screen and type Activate Windows and select the appropriate result. With Windows 10, you can navigate to the options as shown in the steps that follow. Figure 4-1 shows an activated Windows installation and how to get there.

© Joli Ballew 2016
J. Ballew, *Windows To Go*, DOI 10.1007/978-1-4842-2134-1_4

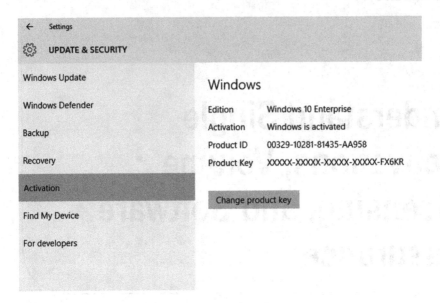

Figure 4-1. *Activate Windows 10 in Settings*

To activate Windows To Go for Windows 10:

1. Click Start.

2. Click Settings.

3. Click Update & Security.

4. Click Activation.

5. If applicable, enter a valid product key.

For any Windows to installation you can view the product key from the Control Panel, as shown in Figure 4-2. You can change the key here should you need to, as well as in Settings shown in Figure 4-1.

Figure 4-2. View the product ID on a Windows 10 machine

What Is Volume Licensing?

It's easy to manage the product ID codes associated with a handful of desktop computers in a small business. It's equally easy to maintain those copies of Windows, reset or refresh computers when necessary, and even troubleshoot problems when they arise. Imagine though if you had, say, 250 computers to manage, or perhaps even thousands. Large businesses that have this kind of environment need a better way to manage their software and licenses, and that's where volume licensing comes in.

Types of Programs

Microsoft Volume Licensing offers lots of licensing programs that businesses can choose from and Microsoft offers several web pages dedicated to choosing the ideal licensing option for specific scenarios. There are multiple solutions, and the right one depends on your company's size and needs. The Volume Licensing solution is an online service. The nice thing about this type of solution is that when businesses acquire software and licenses through the program, there's no need for physical disks or boxes of software to deal with. This, combined with purchasing licenses in volume, reduces the cost for acquiring the software too.

Most of the volume licensing programs that are available come with Software Assurance. This is an additional feature that provides support and maintenance for the software you purchase. Businesses with volume licenses and software assurance can access training and IT tools for administrators, and they have access to partner services and telephone support.

The program you choose depends on several factors, and some thought should go into selecting a program. You'll want to address the size of your organization first and foremost, but you'll also need to consider what type of organization you have. There are many types from small business to large enterprises, as well as educational settings.

You'll also need to consider what kind of software you'll be acquiring licenses for. In this book we're mainly focused on the Windows operating system and perhaps some Microsoft Office software, but there are lots of other pieces of software to consider. Some of those include server operating systems, cloud services, and so on.

Let's look at three types of scenarios: small businesses, midsize and large businesses, and specialized organizations.

■ **Note**   Once you've selected a program and signed up, you'll use the Volume Licensing Service Center (VLSC) to download your products and product keys, and manage what you've purchased. You'll learn more about that later.

Small Business

Small businesses that need five or more licenses, and these can include Windows To Go licenses, can select a version of the Open Value program that meets their needs. There are three options. Two of the three types of these programs include Software Assurance, detailed later in this chapter, and as mentioned already, they offer training and planning support, among other things. This program offers the lowest initial costs and makes it possible to add licenses one at a time if need be. One of the programs waives the five-PC minimum requirement, which makes it more affordable for very small businesses. Let's take a look at the three open license options.

Open License

This program is available for businesses that need to purchase five or more licenses initially, but the regular five licenses is waived in this program to meet the needs of startup companies and extremely small businesses. The Open License program allows businesses the option to add Software Assurance if desired, for an extra fee.

These licensing and assurance options apply to full packaged products and some original equipment manufacturer (OEM) software packages. Pricing is based on the product pools and not on desktop PCs. The agreement term is two years and business have no other option than to pay upfront, and unlike other options, this program option is not renewable. Online Services is offered, which is cloud service that offers productivity software such as Office 365 and Azure.

Open Value

Open Value has similar features as Open License but with a few changes. Software Assurance is included in the price, whereas in the previous program it was an add-on feature. There are no renewal options for OEM software, but renewals are available for licenses and Software Assurance. Unlike the previous program, the five-PC-minimum applies, although discounts are available for companies that apply the program to their entire organization.

This plan's agreement is for three years and is renewable. Both Office 365 and other software are payable annually or upfront in full. As in all three Open plans, Online Services is available.

Open Value Subscription

This final subscription option for small businesses has all of the features of the Open Value program with a few minor changes. The agreement term is only one year for government and educational organizations, and payment is made annually; thus there is no requirement to pay upfront.

■ **Note** To buy or renew one of these program services in the United States, call (800) 426-9400, or find an authorized reseller. In Canada, call the Microsoft Resource Centre at (877) 568-2495. For other countries, visit the Microsoft Volume Licensing web site for your country.

Midsize and Large Businesses

There are more robust solutions for businesses that need more than 250 licenses, such as those found in midsize and large businesses. There are three areas to look at here: the Enterprise agreement, the Microsoft Products and Services agreement, and Select Plus.

Enterprise Agreement

The first of the additional volume licensing agreements to select from is the Enterprise agreement. When compared to buying software using traditional methods, buying in this manner can save a company anywhere from 15 to 45 percent initially. It's a three-year agreement though, so that is certainly something to consider when selecting it; however, you can pay for it annually. You don't have to pay for it all upfront.

With this package you subscribe to Microsoft products instead of owning them. You lease them, so to speak. The same is true of Microsoft services. One of the features of this program is that you can add or remove licenses annually, as the need arises for your particular environment.

There are two types of enrollments: Enterprise and Server and Cloud. Enterprise enrollment offers the best pricing if you're looking to enroll users and devices. Server and Cloud enrollment offers the best pricing if you need to purchase server products and cloud technologies.

■ **Note**   There is a new option for licensing Windows with regard to Software Assurance, with the emphasis on the user. With this option, all of a user's devices are covered, even those running iOS or Android operating system. The only requirement for the user is that the user's primary work PC has to be installed with a valid Windows operating system.

Microsoft Products and Services Agreement

The Microsoft Products and Services Agreement (MPSA) is a broader agreement that can be tailored to three types of organizations: commercial, government, and academic. You can obtain the greatest variety of Microsoft software and services through this type of agreement, and this, like others, includes licenses for Windows To Go drives. The MPSA is the best solution for organizations that want to buy cloud services but don't want to have to buy a license for every person in their company.

Additionally, with this option companies can quickly provision cloud services such as Office 365, Microsoft Azure, Microsoft Intune, or Dynamics CRM Online, among other things. This agreement is flexible, and you can add users and services at any time. You can choose from one-, two-, and three-year agreement durations too.

■ **Note**   Microsoft does not yet provide a specific document where all prices are listed for the MPSA offerings, but prices are provided based on servers, applications, and systems as applicable for a specific organization.

Select Plus

Select Plus is being retired and being replaced with MPSA. However, for companies that still have it, it's available to renew through its next renewal date, starting July 1, 2016. This does not apply to government or academic Select Plus users.

Additional Information about Volume Licensing and Windows To Go

Windows To Go uses volume licensing activation, unless you've acquired an Enterprise edition of Windows and used the Windows To Go Creator to create a single Windows To Go workspace. In an enterprise you can either use Active Directory or Key Management Service (KMS) activation. See the note about KMS. No matter what you select, though, the Windows To Go drives count as a regular installation of Windows and apply to all licensing agreements.

■ **Note** KMS enables organizations to activate Windows systems using their own network. Individual computers don't need to connect to Microsoft to activate when KMS is leveraged. KMS requires a specific number of physical or virtual computers in the company's network environment, which are called minimums or activation thresholds.

If you add software to your Windows image, such as Microsoft Office, and distribute it to Windows To Go workspaces, those pieces of software must also be activated. The same is true of any third-party software you add to the image. Keep this in mind when creating the drive image; purchase licenses as needed.

■ **Caution** It's important to note that Multiple Activation Key (MAK) activation isn't supported with Windows To Go. It shouldn't be used to activate Office or any other software on a Windows To Go drive either.

Software Assurance

You learned earlier that Software Assurance is an option for the Open License plan and included in other volume licensing programs. But what is Software Assurance? Software Assurance is a set of benefits that help you deploy, manage, and use the Microsoft products you own or lease efficiently, and this includes support and training for provisioning and using Windows To Go drives. With regard to Windows and Windows To Go, Software Assurance enables a large business to deliver Windows Enterprise editions across all kinds of devices from virtual machines to Windows To Go workstations.

With Software Assurance you'll also have access to training for your administrators and users. And, of course, you'll have specific Windows and Windows To Go rights, which are discussed next. There are a lot of perks to having Software Assurance, certainly more than are applicable for discussion here, but let's take a look at a few of these in depth as they might apply to Windows To Go.

Windows Version Rights

There are several types of rights associated with Windows and Windows versioning that come with Software Assurance. For one, every license that is covered is available to upgrade to a new version of Windows at no additional cost. You already learned that you can't upgrade a Windows To Go workspace, though, but as it applies to creating those Windows To Go drives, having the ability to upgrade the Windows images you apply is applicable here.

Note that there's no additional cost applied to upgrading Windows when Software Assurance is involved, as there would likely be with an upgrade using a familiar, packaged, off-the-shelf version of Windows.

There are also Virtual Desktop Access rights that enable users to use virtual versions of Windows in an assortment of situations. Of course, there are Windows To Go use rights too. Your employees can use Windows To Go on any device that is licensed under Software Assurance and Volume Licensing.

Additionally, because users roam, Roaming User Rights for Windows enables a user of any Software Assurance licensed device to access a virtual instance of Windows running in a data center. Users can leverage Windows To Go from noncorporate devices too, including their own PCs, public computers, and any other device that allows for booting to the workspace. Having this ability is central to using Windows To Go effectively, as you well know.

Technical and End-User Training

Software Assurance benefits include training for Windows software and services, cloud services, deployment and management, and more, from a benefit product catalogue available at the web site shown in Figure 4-3. Training is available 24 hours a day, 7 days a week for Software Assurance customers.

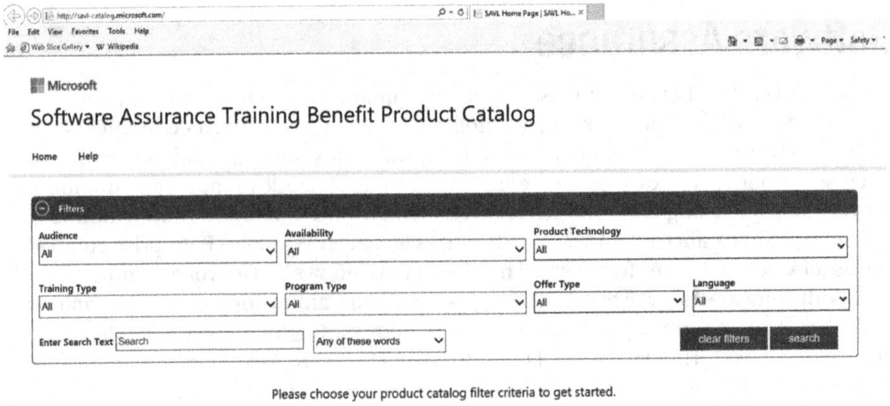

Figure 4-3. *Access Software Assurance training*

As you might imagine, there are lots of kinds of training available. You can get classroom training from a live instructor through your local Microsoft Learning Partner. The instructors are Microsoft Certified Trainers (MCT). These trainers have to undergo rigorous training themselves, as well as pass applicable tests to earn this certification and ultimately teach courses.

To find a learning partner, visit the web site shown in Figure 4-4, type your criteria, and click Search.

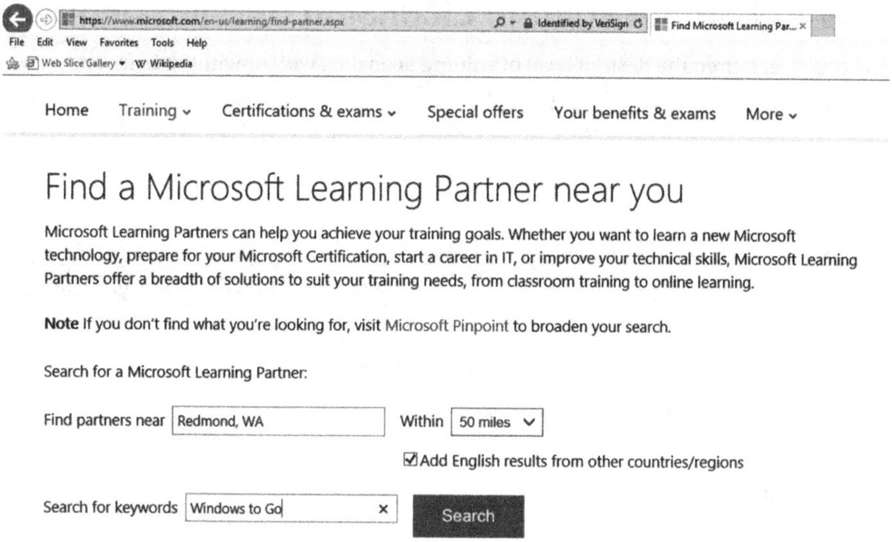

Figure 4-4. Locate a Microsoft Learning Partner

With regard to classroom training, users enroll for training using training vouchers. Eligible courses are those that are deemed Microsoft Official Courseware (designed for IT professionals or developers) and do not include training for Excel, Word, and PowerPoint or hands-on labs, first-look clinics, or Microsoft Press books.

■ **Note** You must access training vouchers before your Software Assurance coverage expires. The voucher remains valid for 180 days after the date you acquired it, and it needs to be used within that time frame.

Users can also access training with self-paced training delivered over the Internet, or if applicable, over a company's own intranet. This is called e-Learning. Because the training is available from Microsoft via Software Assurance, training won't impact a company's budget. There are as many options for e-learning as there are users with Software Assurance licenses, and those users can access training for the product they use (such as Windows 10 Enterprise).

How to Use the Volume Licensing Service Center

One you've acquired the desired level of volume licensing, with or without Software Assurance, you manage those licenses from the VLSC, shown in Figure 4-5. You can also download software here, view the details of your account, and even grant permissions.

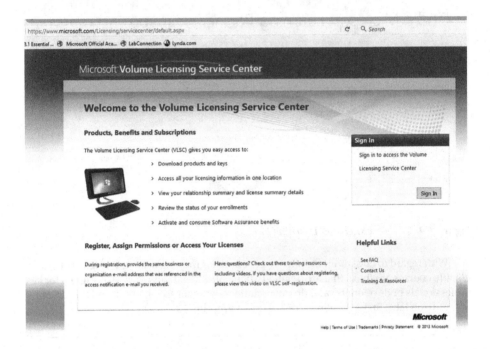

Figure 4-5. *Use the Volume Licensing Service Center to manage volume licenses*

To use the VLSC you must first sign in. You can see the sign-in link in Figure 4-5. Once you're in, you'll see various tabs across the top including but not limited to Home, Licenses, Downloads and Keys, Software Assurance, Administration, and Help.

Figure 4-6 shows the Home tab. As you can see, there are quick links to software downloads and keys, online activation, and license summary, and a link to add an open license, as applicable.

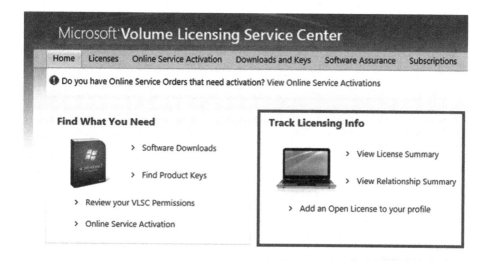

Figure 4-6. *Use the Home tab of the VLSC to access quick links to common tasks*

■ **Note**   Microsoft will require both a Windows Live ID and a valid business e-mail address to ensure secure access to licensing data.

Here are a few other quick tips for using this portal:

- Use the Licenses tab to view license versions and quantities.

- From the Downloads and Keys page, you can access your products.

- From the Software Assurance page, review your benefits.

- From the subscriptions page access MSDN or TechNet subscriptions, among other things.

- From the Help tab access help.

Summary

To use Windows To Go in an enterprise you'll need to manage the licenses for it using the same techniques you use to manage regular Windows licenses. You do this through volume licensing. There are many licensing programs to choose from, and you'll choose the one that is right for you based on the size of your company and type of organization. Once signed up you'll use the VLSC to manage licenses as well as any Software Assurance benefits you own. In Chapter 5 you'll learn how to deploy Windows To Go drives.

CHAPTER 5

■ ■ ■

Deploy Windows To Go Drives

So far you've learned about provisioning single Windows To Go drives for exploration and single-use scenarios, you've looked at the requirements for creating and offering those drives in a small to medium-sized business, and you've explored a little about how it all works in an enterprise, including some steps to take on your servers to start the planning and prepping process. In this chapter you'll learn more about how it all works in an enterprise, including what needs to be considered and how to actually create the images you'll use once you have all of the pieces in place.

You might use a Windows Deployment Services server to do this. You might opt to automate the process for self-provisioning using System Center. Or, you might use what you already have in place to create and modify images, such DISM, and then deploy those images using PowerShell. There are lots of ways to go, and I suggest looking at what's already in place in your enterprise before you commit to any one solution.

That said, you likely won't put what's required to create, capture, and deploy drives in place just to create 20 or 30 Windows To Go drives. You could create each manually using other options, including third-party cloning tools. It's far more likely you already have a process for creating and managing Windows images, and you need to add this to your existing Windows program. With that in mind, then, know that I won't walk you through the entire process here, from start to finish. That's a book all in itself. However, I can guide you through the general steps you'll need to navigate to get from where you are now to provisioning Windows To Go drives in your enterprise, giving you lots of options in the process.

■ **Note** Before we dive in, make sure you understand that in an enterprise you capture and create the images that you'll use on Windows To Go drives the same way you capture and create regular Windows images for your laptops and desktops.

© Joli Ballew 2016
J. Ballew, *Windows To Go*, DOI 10.1007/978-1-4842-2134-1_5

Considerations for Deployment

The initial need for Windows To Go came about as users in medium- to large-sized businesses started to become more mobile, both in the field and in the office. There needed to be a solution to let these users work even when a computer wasn't available. As this need expanded and technologies started forming around these new scenarios, enterprises embraced Windows To Go as a valid option for solving some of their mobile problems. What they wanted and needed, though, was for their users to have the same experience on their Windows To Go drives as they would have if they were actually sitting at a corporate machine, at a desk, in a cubicle, doing traditional work. This had to be part of the solution.

Thus, from the onset, Microsoft created Windows To Go to mimic a user's corporate desktop experience. Microsoft wanted to make the drives easy to provision too, and to allow companies to use the infrastructure already in place to minimize additional costs or training. To make this happen, Windows To Go drives had to be able to be both compatible with existing deployment workflows and have the ability take on corporate Windows images that had already been created by corporations. Of course, limiting cost is a factor too, and thus Windows To Go drives had to be both available and affordable. Compatible drives are inexpensive, adding to the Windows To Go solution.

In this part of the chapter I'll offer information about some things to consider as you get ready for your capture and deployment tasks. Let's start with some basics of using Windows images.

Windows Images

As noted, if you're in an enterprise environment, you likely already have a plan in place to create and modify your own custom Windows images. Before you start the process though, let's take at the requirements to make sure you have met them. The process will go a lot more smoothly if you don't have to stop and put something new into place.

If you're planning on performing these tasks with Microsoft products using an in-house workflow, you need, among other things:

- An existing deployment infrastructure that includes administrative rights to the computers and servers you'll use to create and manage images, the Windows Application and Deployment Toolkit (ADK), and a Windows Preinstallation Environment (Windows PE) disk.

- System Center 2012 Configuration Manager SP1 or later to enable users to self-provision Windows To Go drives.

- Blank USB drives that are Windows To Go compatible and are at least 32 GB.

- A basic or custom .WIM or .iso image.

- Applicable device drivers.

- A way to copy the image to the physical Windows To Go device, which can include USB ports, USB duplicators, and so on.

Once you've created the image, and you'll learn how in this chapter, you can duplicate that image as many times as you like, provided you select an applicable type of image. Image types are outlined in the section Leverage Existing Infrastructure later in this chapter. Note that although images are reusable from the creator standpoint, once an image is deployed to a specific USB drive, that image is "used up." You can't reuse that image again; you'll always use the original Windows image you create employing the tools outlined in this chapter.

■ **Note**   If you use a USB drive duplicator to duplicate Windows To Go drives, do not configure offline domain join or BitLocker on the Windows To Go drive image.

Driver Considerations

A device driver is a piece of software that lets software talk to hardware. In the case of Windows To Go, you need the applicable device drivers to allow the Windows To Go device to communicate with the host computer. Because there are so many different computer manufacturers and hardware combinations, though, some thought needs to go into adding the required drivers to the Windows To Go images you create. As you'd suspect, you add those drivers prior to deployment and during image creation.

You might know that Windows includes a driver store that holds device drivers that can support a variety of computers and peripherals already. When you connect a computer to a new piece of hardware such as a printer, or when you boot a Windows To Go drive with a computer you've never booted to before, drivers are automatically loaded for all of the new devices it discovers. The drivers available in the default Driver Store that comes with Windows might work just fine. Most of the time the files required by computers and Windows To Go are in this repository. However, if they aren't, Windows will look to Windows Update, again providing a safety net should you not include everything you need. This is true for both external and internal devices. In both Windows and Windows To Go, the driver store is located under **\Windows\System32\ DriverStore\File Repository** as shown in Figure 5-1.

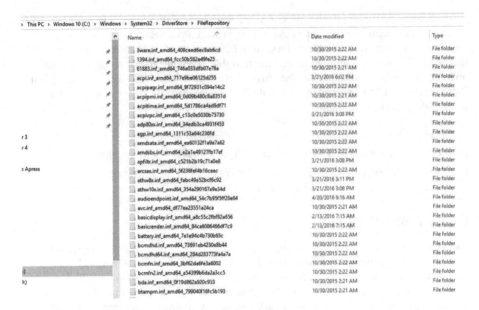

> This PC > Windows 10 (C:) > Windows > System32 > DriverStore > FileRepository

Name	Date modified	Type
3ware.inf_amd64_408ceed6ec8ab6cd	10/30/2015 2:22 AM	File folder
1394.inf_amd64_fcc50b582e49fe25	10/30/2015 2:22 AM	File folder
61883.inf_amd64_746a033dfb07e78a	10/30/2015 2:21 AM	File folder
acpi.inf_amd64_717e9be06125d255	3/21/2016 6:02 PM	File folder
acpipagr.inf_amd64_9f72931c094a14c2	10/30/2015 2:22 AM	File folder
acpipmi.inf_amd64_0d09b480c8a8351d	10/30/2015 2:21 AM	File folder
acpitime.inf_amd64_5d1786ca4ad9df71	10/30/2015 2:22 AM	File folder
acpivpc.inf_amd64_c13c0e5030b73730	3/21/2016 3:08 PM	File folder
adp80xx.inf_amd64_34edb3ca4931f453	10/30/2015 2:22 AM	File folder
agp.inf_amd64_1311c53a64c236fd	10/30/2015 2:22 AM	File folder
amdsata.inf_amd64_ea60132f1a9a7a62	10/30/2015 2:22 AM	File folder
amdsbs.inf_amd64_e2a1e49127fb17ef	10/30/2015 2:22 AM	File folder
apfiltr.inf_amd64_c521b2b19c71a0e8	3/21/2016 3:08 PM	File folder
arcsas.inf_amd64_5f236fef4b16ceac	10/30/2015 2:22 AM	File folder
athw8x.inf_amd64_fabc49a52bcf6c92	3/21/2016 3:11 PM	File folder
athw10x.inf_amd64_354a290167a9e34d	3/21/2016 3:08 PM	File folder
audioendpoint.inf_amd64_54c7b95f5ff28e64	4/20/2016 9:16 AM	File folder
avc.inf_amd64_df77ea23551a24ca	10/30/2015 2:21 AM	File folder
basicdisplay.inf_amd64_a8c55c2fbf82a656	2/13/2016 7:15 AM	File folder
basicrender.inf_amd64_84ca6086466df7c9	2/13/2016 7:15 AM	File folder
battery.inf_amd64_7e1e94c4b730b65c	10/30/2015 2:22 AM	File folder
bcmdhd.inf_amd64_73691eb4230e8b44	10/30/2015 2:22 AM	File folder
bcmdhd64.inf_amd64_284d283773fa4a7a	10/30/2015 2:22 AM	File folder
bcmfn.inf_amd64_3bf62da6fe3a6002	10/30/2015 2:22 AM	File folder
bcmfn2.inf_amd64_a54399b6da2a3cc5	10/30/2015 2:22 AM	File folder
bda.inf_amd64_0f19d862a920c933	10/30/2015 2:21 AM	File folder
btampm.inf_amd64_799040f16fc5b193	10/30/2015 2:21 AM	File folder

Figure 5-1. *The Driver Store is included in all Windows images*

With regard to images you create for Windows To Go drives, you'll want to add any images to Windows that aren't included here that you think you might need. For instance, if you know you'll be using the Windows To Go workspaces on a specific set of computers that has specialty hardware not normally found inside a computer tower, you can incorporate the drivers for those computers into the image you create.

You should make a special effort to also add any network-related drivers too, including Wi-Fi drivers. It's very important that Windows To Go drives be able to connect to the Internet through their host. They need access to Windows Update as well as to your corporate domain, they need access to the Internet to activate successfully on first use, and so on.

Domain Join

You will either deploy the Windows To Go drives to users while they are on company property (at work) or you will give a Windows To Go drives to users to set up when they are away from the office. However you decide to do it, the user needs some way to join the domain, and this needs to be set up beforehand as part of the image you create. How the user joins this domain varies, but there are a few options you should consider and put into practice prior to actually handing over a drive to a user.

At work, joining a domain is generally achieved the same way it is when a laptop or desktop is provisioned to a new user. The user with the Windows To Go drive first works through any setup processes and then connects to the enterprise network. Generally, a user receives an IP (Internet Protocol) address via DHCP (Dynamic Host Configuration Protocol). Once connected, the user's group policies are applied (at least those that aren't included in the image), BitLocker keys are stored in the applicable Active Directory Domain Services area, and the user is connected to network resources. If there's anything else that needs to happen, like getting software, accessing online applications, updating the software installed, and accessing personal data online or in the domain, it happens after this.

If you plan to deploy a Windows To Go drive to a user who isn't going to be at work when he or she initializes the drive, you'll need to make sure that you configure offline domain join and BitLocker. You'll also need to consider how the user will actually connect, perhaps via a VPN (Virtual Private Network) or DirectAccess. This and other initialization tasks should be considered and incorporated before giving the drive to the user.

■ **Note** To learn more about Remote Access options review the document Deploy Remote Access in an Enterprise, available at TechNet.

Install Applications

If you have an infrastructure in place that you can use to create unattended Windows installations, you can create your Windows To Go drives so that end users don't have to do much of anything the first time they use them. With Windows To Go there is something similar called self-provisioning, which is detailed later in this chapter in the section titled Use System Center. However, most enterprises don't have this type of infrastructure, so the first time a user initializes a drive he or she will have a bit of work to do. This can include more than just working through a short setup process and joining the domain. It can also include installing applications or, at least, updating them.

Figure 5-2 shows a prompt a user might receive after booting Windows To Go the first time. It states that updates are available. This is a common prompt so you'll want to train your users appropriately before you hand over a drive. As with any Windows deployment, you'll have to put a plan in place to incorporate installations or updates. If possible it's best to put the updates into the image prior to creating the drives.

Figure 5-2. A user might be prompted to perform his or her own updates

If users need to get something at the Windows Store, it's certainly possible with Windows 8.1 and 10. There are limitations on the store for Windows 8, as noted in Chapter 1. You'll need to teach users how to do that, and, you'll need to allow them to get to the store. So, you'll want to enable the Windows Store during the image creation process; if you don't know, it's disabled by default. You can enable this in your domain Group Policy or in Local Group Policy.

Here's how to enable the Store using a Local Group Policy editor:

1. Use the Windows +R key to open a Run box.

2. Type gpedit.msc and hit Enter on the keyboard.

3. Navigate to **Computer Configuration\Administrative templates\Windows Components\Store.**

4. Double click "**Allow Store to install apps on Windows To Go workspaces**" policy.

5. Click Enable.

6. Click Apply, then OK.

7. Click the Windows key + R to open a Run dialog box.

8. Type CMD and press Enter.

9. Type **gpupdate/force** and click Enter to apply the changes immediately. See Figure 5-3.

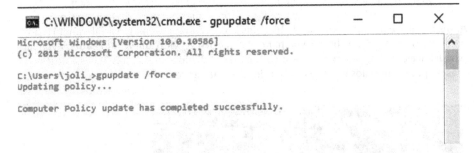

*Figure 5-3. Apply the new policy immediately using the **gpudpate /force** command; if you don't, the policy won't be applied until Group Policy updates again on its own*

10. Close the command prompt window.

Finally, although you might host applications on site and let users access applications remotely, they could instead be in charge of working through an installation process themselves from a startup script or through the actual application. Figure 5-4 shows a prompt users could see after installing and then updating Microsoft Office.

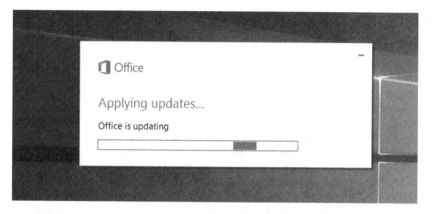

Figure 5-4. *Users might need to work through an update process*

However you opt to get software to users, make sure to train them in installation and update procedures. Make as much of it as possible user-friendly too. In a best-case scenario users would not need to install anything, but this isn't often possible.

Apply Group Policy

You already applied Group Policies to your domain enterprise users, and you can apply the same policies to your Windows To Go users. You learned about this in Chapter 3. However, there are a few policy settings that are Windows To Go-specific. Although we touched on these in an earlier chapter, let's take one more look to refresh your memory, and look at them in a little more depth.

The specific Windows To Go Group Policy settings are located at **Computer Configuration\Administrative Templates\Windows Components\Portable Operating System** in the Local Group Policy Editor. See Figure 5-5.

Figure 5-5. *Configure Group Policies that are Windows To Go-specific*

Allow Hibernate (S4) When Started from a Windows To Go workspace

This policy setting specifies whether the PC can use the hibernation sleep state (S4) when started from a Windows To Go workspace. By default, hibernation is disabled when using a Windows To Go workspace because when a computer enters hibernation, the contents of memory are written to disk. When the disk is resumed, the hardware must still be available to provide the information to the operating system. Oftentimes, the Windows To Go drive would not be booted to the same host it would have hibernated to; this would ultimately cause a loss of data. Also, the Windows To Go drive would have to be connected to the same USB port it was connected to when it went into hibernation. Even if the same host is used, it is possible that a different USB port would be used, and that would imply that the Windows To Go drive had been removed anyway, and reinserted. All of this would cause data loss if the drive were configured to go into hibernation on a host.

For these reasons and others, hibernation is not recommended for Windows To Go drives. Hibernation should only be used when you are positive that the Windows To Go workspace is always used on the same PC and does not roam.

Disallow Standby Sleep States (S1-S3) When Starting from a Windows To Go Workspace

This policy setting specifies whether the PC can use standby sleep states (S1–S3) when started from a Windows To Go workspace. The sleep state is not enabled by default, because when a computer goes to sleep, it appears as though the computer and Windows To Go are both shut down. A user might think that both were shut down properly, when in reality they were not. Because shutting down a Windows To Go drive incorrectly by removing it before it has been properly shut down can harm or corrupt the drive, it's best to leave this feature disabled.

Windows To Go Default Startup Options

This policy setting controls whether the host computer will boot to Windows To Go if a USB a Windows To Go drive is connected. It also controls whether users can make changes to the Windows To Go Startup Options settings dialog. Note that if you enable this setting it will cause PCs running Windows to attempt to boot from any USB device that is inserted into the PC before it is started, not just Windows To Go devices.

Bios and Firmware

Speaking of host computers and Windows To Go startup options, you learned earlier, and it makes sense, that the biggest problem users have with Windows To Go is the boot process. That process depends on the type of machine, its configuration, how its BIOS and boot order are configured, and so on. If a computer hasn't previously been configured to boot to Windows To Go a user might attempt to enter the BIOS options himself to change it. This could result in many types of failures, including making the host computer completely unbootable. Because of this it's necessary that you try very hard to reduce the number of situations during boot that users might experience and try to fix themselves. With that in mind you should always enable the Windows To Go startup options to allow for Windows To Go boot-ups beforehand. With this done there's no need to worry about firmware or BIOS or users trying to configure these options themselves.

You learned how to perform this task in Chapter 1 and you can enable it in Group Policy as outlined previously. Figure 5-6 shows the dialog box for making the change on a single PC using the graphical end-user interface.

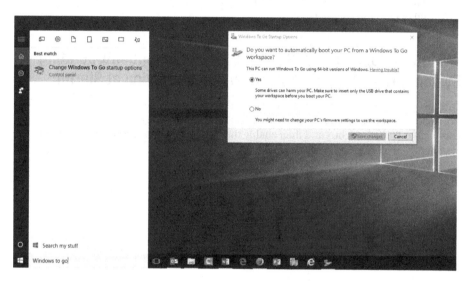

Figure 5-6. *Configure Windows To Go startup options on a Windows 10 computer*

Regarding firmware, Windows supports two types: Unified Extensible Firmware Interface (UEFI) and legacy BIOS firmware. BIOS was used frequently with Windows 7 PCs and earlier, and most Windows 8 and windows 10 PCs use UEFI. Windows To Go supports both, and when you create a Windows To Go drive using the Windows To Go Creator or using any existing infrastructure for applying images in an enterprise, that support is built in. However, if you are planning to use Windows To Go drives manually you must use the ALL parameter to provide the Windows To Go drive the ability to boot on both types of firmware. For example, on volume F: (your Windows To Go USB drive letter), you would use the command **bcdboot C:\windows /s F: /f ALL**.

Enable BitLocker

You know about BitLocker and how it protects the Windows To Go drive. You'll want to enable BitLocker on your drives to protect them. You can choose to enable BitLocker protection on Windows To Go drives beforehand as part of the provisioning process, which ensures the process completes successfully and enables for a faster encryption process, or you can allow your end users to apply BitLocker protection themselves, during their own initialization processes. If you opt to apply BitLocker beforehand, you'll need some way to get that BitLocker password to the user and tell him to change his password immediately at first use.

You'll also need a plan in place to store and recover BitLocker recovery keys. These keys can unlock the drive when the user forgets the passcode or some other problem arises. You should back up these keys to Active Directory Domain Services (ADDS), although you can have users store keys in the cloud, on a USB drive, or on a network drive. They'll be prompted to do so during the creation.

There are also a few Group Policy settings to consider prior to making decisions about BitLocker, which I'll detail next.

\Windows Components\BitLocker Drive Encryption\Operating System Drives\Require Additional Authentication at Startup

You have to enable this policy if the computer does not have a TPM chip, which USB drives do not. You must enable this setting and select Allow BitLocker without a compatible TPM check box and then enable the Configure use of passwords for operating system drives setting. See Figure 5-7.

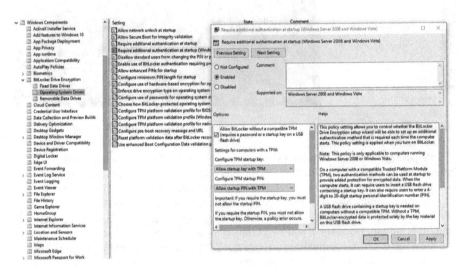

Figure 5-7. *Enable the option to allow BitLocker without a TPM*

\Windows Components\BitLocker Drive Encryption\Operating System Drives\Configure Use of Passwords for Operating System Drives

This policy setting enables passwords to be used to unlock BitLocker-protected operating system drives. See Figure 5-8. You can also configure complexity and length requirements on passwords for Windows To Go workspaces. If you enable these settings you should also enable the Group Policy setting "Password must meet complexity requirements" located in **Computer Configuration\Windows Settings\Security Settings\Account Policies\Password Policy**.

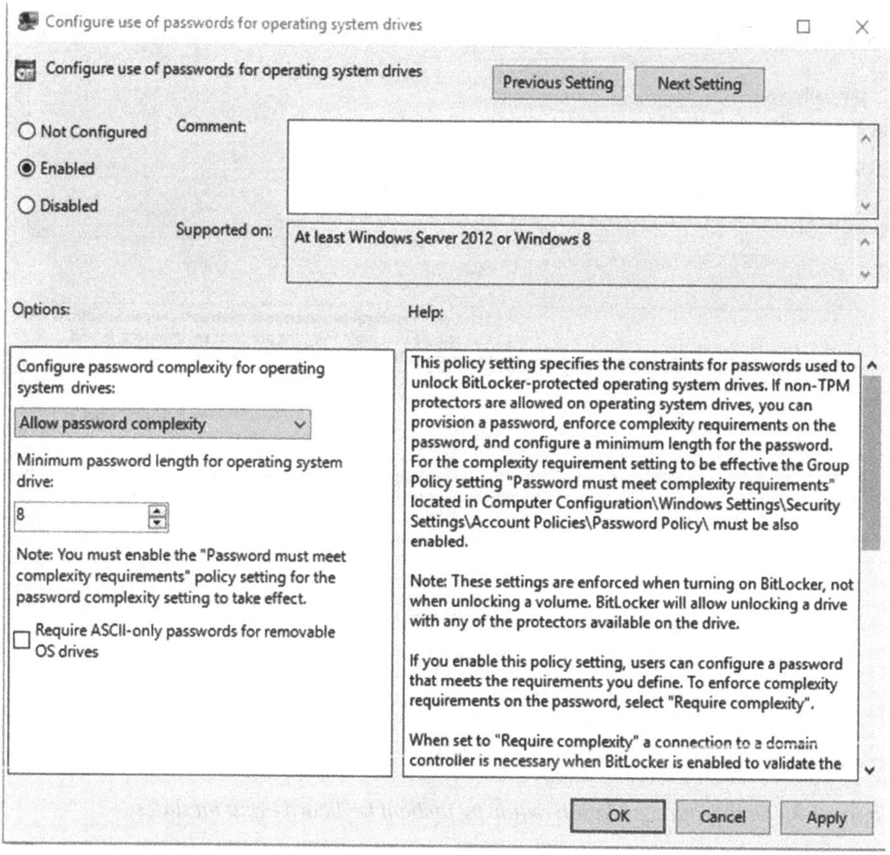

Figure 5-8. *Configure use of passwords*

\Windows Components\BitLocker Drive Encryption\Operating System Drives\Enable Use of BitLocker Authentication Requiring Preboot Keyboard Input on Slates

This policy setting allows users to enable authentication options that require user input from the preboot environment even if the drive doesn't provide preboot input capability. You must enable this setting if you want passwords to be used to unlock BitLocker-protected operating system drives. See Figure 5-9.

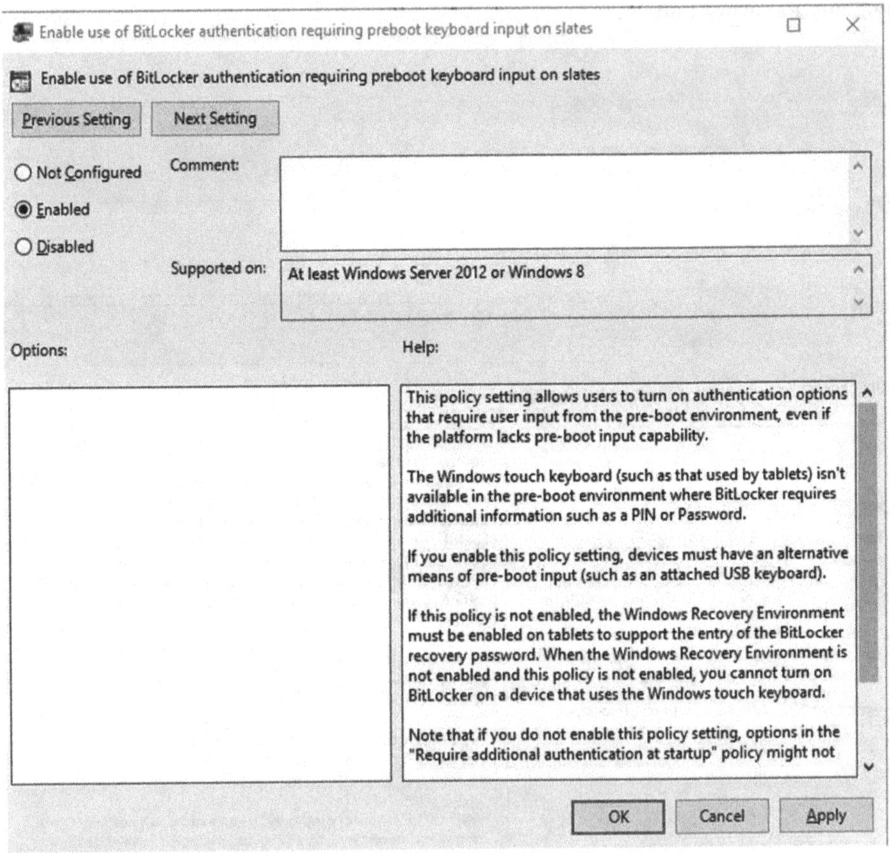

Figure 5-9. Enable authentication requiring preboot keyboard input on slates

Deploy Windows To Go with PowerShell

If you only need to create a few Windows To Go drives you can use the Windows To Go creator to create them one at a time. If you have say, 100 drives to create and already have a workflow and infrastructure in place for creating Windows images, you can us that workflow to create the drives. If the latter is the case, there's no need for me to rehash what you already have and know, especially if you already have an IT department that's knowledgeable about such things. However, if you're looking for something new or you are just getting going with Windows To Go, you might be interested in creating drives using PowerShell scripts. That's what I'd like to talk about here.

■ **Note**   PowerShell administrators generally deploy Windows To Go to multiple devices using the technique outlined here.

As you might imagine, it would be difficult for me to create and type a script here that could be applied to scenarios to create drives and deploy them that work for all readers, but lucky for us, Microsoft offers sample deployment scripts free of change at its TechNet web site. To see this script and information about how to use it, locate the web page shown in Figure 5-10. You can find it by searching for Deploy Windows To Go, Technet, from any web browser.

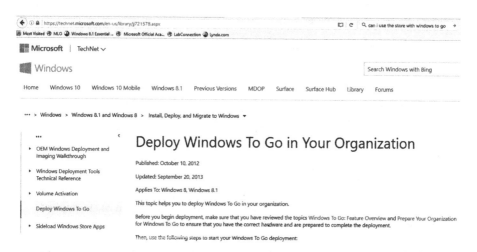

Figure 5-10. *Use the sample deployment scripts available from TechNet to deploy Windows To Go*

Once at the page, scroll down to the Advanced Deployment Sample Scripts area. Note that although this webpage applies to Windows 8, you can adapt it to work for Windows 10 and your environment where applicable. You learned in the last chapter what needs to be updated in any infrastructure to create Windows To Go drives, so if you have any questions return there before copying the scripts here.

From the sample script area you can locate and copy a script to use in PowerShell to provision multiple Windows To Go drives and to also configure offline domain join. Before you start to use this script, note these requirements:

- From a domain-joined computer, open a Windows PowerShell session as an administrator.

- The administrator account you use must have permission to create domain accounts.

- You can only provision half as many drives as you have drive letters, which is a limitation of the sample script you're learning about here.

- If you are using DirectAccess you'll need to modify the djoin. exe command to include policy names and potentially the certtemplate parameters.

To run the advanced deployment sample script:

1. From this web page, locate and then copy the entire the code sample titled "Windows To Go multiple drive provisioning sample script" into a PowerShell script (.ps1) file.

2. Paste the file into Notepad or something similar.

3. Make the required modifications to make it an appropriate script for your deployment and save the file.

4. From an elevated PowerShell prompt type Set-ExecutionPolicy RemoteSigned.

5. Run the script.

During this process, the PowerShell script will try to detect the drives that are connected to the machine you're working on, specifically USB drives that can be provisioned with Windows To Go that are larger than 20 GB. (As with other parameters, you can modify this number before running the script.) After that you'll verify that you want to clear the contents of these drives, which means any existing data will be removed. There will be two partitions created to support both UEFI and BIOS host machines during this process and all soon-to-be Windows To Go drives will be formatted.

During the process as outlined in this script, BitLocker encryption will be applied and unique recovery keys will be created. You'll need to decide where to store those keys, and Active Directory is the best option; however, you can use other options. Whatever the case, you'll need to copy the key during this process. BitLocker applied in this manner is a great way to go because only the used space on the drive is encrypted during this process, which makes the process go a lot faster. As data is added by the user, that data will subsequently be encrypted as well.

Now you'll apply your image. You'll need to select the enterprise image that you want to use for Windows To Go. You might need to change the Index entry here. You do this by modifying the provided DISM command.

Finally, you'll add the boot files. If you want to roam with the drive you'll want to put all available files there. If you want to, you can now append other files like unattend files, additional policy files, and so forth.

Note that you can get more information about this sample script and locate others on TechNet, MSDN, and other Microsoft-supported areas of the Web. There are third-party scripts available too, and often you can reach out to the manufacturers of your Windows To Go compatible drives for help as well.

Leverage Existing Infrastructure

In this section I'll go over a few items related to existing infrastructure. You know already that Windows To Go makes it possible to use existing infrastructure to work with these workspaces. So, in this part of the chapter I'll talk a little about the types of images you might already have and want to work with, including disk, sector, file, and Windows Image Format files. I'll include information about how those files come to be, and their advantages and disadvantages. The idea here is that if you have existing infrastructure in place, you can use it with Windows To Go.

Types of Images

If you already have images available to you that you'd like to use on Windows To Go drives, you can certainly opt to use them. However, if you think you might want to consider other options, there are four types of images to contemplate: disk images, sector-based images, file-based images, and Windows Imaging Format (WIM) images.

Disk and Sector-Based Images

A disk image is a single file that contains an entire disk structure and thus includes a lot more data than just a single copy of Windows. It can also include applications, drivers, Windows updates, software updates, and even settings like desktop backgrounds and screensavers. The image is generally created in enterprises by installing Windows on a reference computer, configuring it to one's liking, and then making a copy of the disk. This image is then saved to a network location as a complete installation package that can be used to install computers.

Disk images can be used to create VHDs. These images can also be burned to a CD or DVD. They can also be used as system backups and data recovery (if created in the appropriate manner). Because the disk image is a copy of an entire disk, though, the file can be quite large. You can see an example of a disk image file in Figure 5-11.

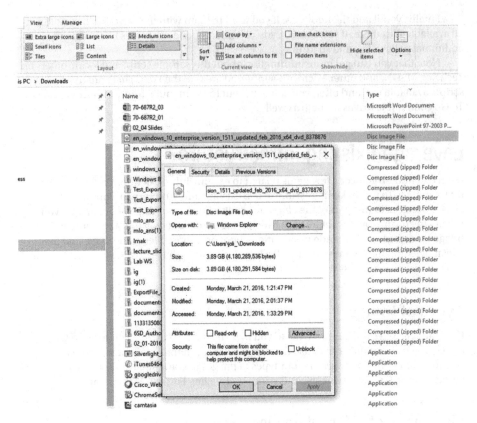

Figure 5-11. *A disk image file is often quite large*

Here I've navigated to the Downloads folder and am viewing by Details. This figure also shows the properties sheet for a Windows 10 disk image file, and note that this one has an .iso extension.

ISO images are sector-based. When you use a sector-based image to deploy Windows you have to take care to remove the original computer name and the security identifier (SID). These two items uniquely identify the computer on which is was created. Sector-based images can be a bad choice if you want to use the image on computers with varying hardware that might conflict with the image created, unless you have an option available to remove this information.

File-Based Disk Images and WIM

A file-based image is one that is captured based on actual files on a disk and is thus not a complete copy of the disk itself. These images are not based on any sort of hardware; they are only based on actual files. Thus, they are hardware-independent and can be deployed to almost any Windows-compatible computer hardware. This is also a single file like a sector-based file, and it remains intact after use, so it can be used over and over and deployed to hundreds of computers.

File-based images are often created as WIM files. You used to use ImageX, part of the Windows Automated Installation Kit (WAIK) and the ADK, to create WIM files. ImageX has been deprecated now though, and has been replaced with DISM. Administrators use DISM to install, uninstall, configure, modify, and update Windows features, packages, drivers, and so on in an existing .wim file or VHD. To make these modifications they use the available DISM servicing commands, some of which are detailed in the section titled Manually Capture the Image with DISM later in this chapter. DISM was introduced in Windows 7 and Server 2008 R2.

WIM files offer the following advantages over other file formats as they relates to enterprises and Windows To Go:

- You can include multiple images.

- You can compress the file.

- The components of the file are hardware independent.

- The file supports offline servicing (you can open a .WIM file and add or remove folders, files, drivers, and so on).

- You can use DISM to modify the file.

Capture Images

To create an image that you can use to deploy to Windows To Go devices you must first configure an image. To do this, you create a reference computer that incorporates everything you want to include with the image. It should contain the operating system, of course, but it might also contain applications and drivers. It can also contain specific settings and even policies you want applied on first use.

Once the computer is set up exactly as you want it, you use the Sysprep command-line tool to prepare it for cloning. Sysprep is outlined next.

Use Sysprep.exe

Sysprep prepares a computer for imaging by removing unique identifiers from the image before creation. You have to do this to be able to reuse that image on different computers. Specifically it's the **sysprep /generalize** command that removes this information, which is data that is on the computer that is specific to the reference computer's installation like the security indentifier, system restore points, event logs, and so on. This is a required step in preparing the Windows installation so that it can be successfully imaged. After applying this command with other applicable parameters, on reboot, a new security identifier is created, activation is reset, and other tasks are performed.

The sysprep.exe command has other parameters beyond /Generalize though. They are shown in Table 5-1.

Table 5-1. Sysprep.exe Parameters

Command	Description
/audit	Lets you add additional drivers or applications to Windows.
/OOBE	Restarts the computer in Windows Welcome mode to let users customize their own OS with user names and other settings.
/Reboot	Restarts the computer to ensure everything works properly.
/Shutdown	Shuts down the computer after Sysprep completes.
/Quiet	Use if you automate Sysprep; it stops any display of messages and confirmations.
/Quit	Closes Sysprep after running commands.
/Unattend	Applies settings specified in an answer file, if one is created. You must specify the path.

■ **Note** A Sysprep command might look like this: **sysprep.exe [/oobe | /audit]** **[/generalize] [/reboot | /shutdown | /quit] [/quiet] [/unattend:***answerfile***]**.

Manually Capture the Image with DISM

After you've run the Sysprep command you are ready to capture the image. You can do that with DISM (among other ways), which is available in the Windows ADK. You'll need a Windows PE disk, which you can create with the Windows ADK as well.

To create a Windows PE disk:

1. Open the **Deployment and Imaging Tools Environment** as an **administrator**. See Figure 5-12.

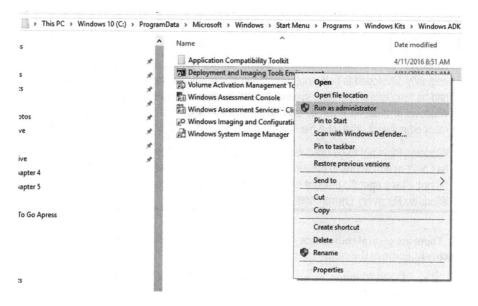

Figure 5-12. Run the Deployment and Imaging Tools Environment as an administrator

2. At the command prompt, type copype amd64 C:\WinPE_
    amd64 using parameter edits as applicable. Press Enter.

3. Then type MakeWinPEMedia/UFD c:\WinPE_amd64 F: using
    parameters as applicable. Press Enter.

With the PE disk created, you can now work through the following steps, which are
detailed broadly:

1. Put the Windows PE disk in the applicable drive or port.

2. Restart the computer and boot to the Windows PE disk.

3. Map a drive to a network share.

4. Use the DiskPart command to assign a drive letter to the
    partitions you need to capture if they do not have drive letters
    associated with them.

5. Use DISM to capture the system partition, if it's been
    customized. Note the DISM command listed below.

6. Use DISM to capture the other partitions including the
    primary partition and any logical partitions.

WHAT IS WINDOWS PE?

Windows PE is a Windows operating system with limited capabilities that was originally developed to help original equipment manufacturers boot machines that had no functioning operating system. It can also be used to prepare a computer for Windows installation. It can be used to copy disk images from a network share or mapped network drive, or a file service. It can also be used to initiate Windows Setup.

Windows PE is not to be used as the primary operating system on a computer, and it has built-in limitations to prevent that—including limited resources and a scheduled reboot after a specific amount of time has passed. It can also be used to initiate the Windows Recovery Environment (Windows RE).

There are several commands you'll need to become familiar with to use DISM effectively. Some of the commands include:

- DISM /Capture-Image — with applicable parameters that name the image file and location for all applicable partitions.

- DISM /Capture-Image — with applicable parameters that specify the location of the configuration file, whether to compress the file, to make a volume image a bootable image, to check for errors, and so on.

- Net Use — to create a network share to store the image and to access that image later.

- Copy — to copy the image files to the network share.

With the image created, you are now ready to deploy. You can use your existing infrastructure to do that, if you already have a plan and workflow in place. You can deploy with PowerShell, detailed earlier, and you can use System Center, detailed next, if your enterprise supports this technology.

Use System Center

You can let users self-provision their own Windows To Go drives if you have access to System Center. Using this technology, administrators can create task sequences to support automating Windows To Go deployments and allow those deployments to be initiated by end users. You do this by prestaging the media using System Center's Configuration Manager.

In broad terms, the process goes like this:

1. An administrator sets up System Center Configuration Manager to create the content for the deployment package.

2. The Configuration Manager offers a wizard to assist in the process. The wizard helps you create a deployment package that contains the operating system package, boot images to support all architectures, applications, drivers, and so on.

3. The package can contain a BitLocker pin, BitLocker requirements, BitLocker policies, and so on.

4. The wizard assists in naming a place where recovery keys will be stored.

5. The wizard helps you to name a distribution point to hold the completed package.

6. Toward the end of the wizard you are prompted to add device drivers as applicable.

7. The wizard lets you point to any answer files you've created to further automate the process and require as little from the end user as possible.

8. Finally, the wizard helps you create the prestaged WIM file and also attach the Creator tool. All of this is collected in a single source directory.

With the entire package available in an online store or application portal as applicable to your enterprise, users now visit the specified area to create their own Windows To Go drives. They insert the drive into their own computer, navigate to the store, and click Install, and the Windows To Go Creator starts. It looks like the Windows To Go Creator you've already seen, and users only need to work through a few clicks to create a drive. If you've forgotten what that tool looks like, it's shown in Figure 5-13.

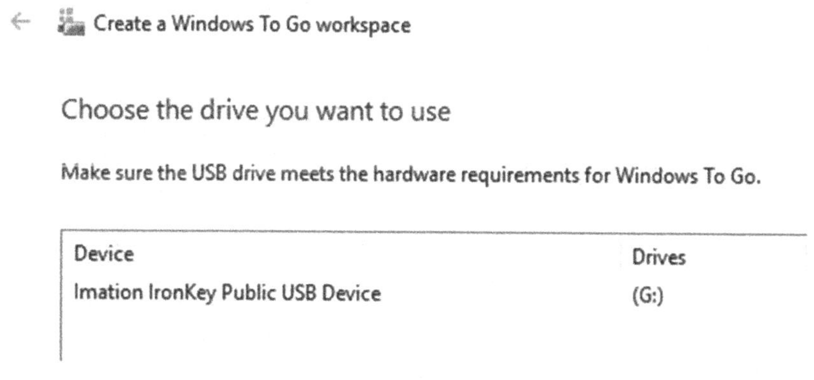

← ⁞▦ Create a Windows To Go workspace

Choose the drive you want to use

Make sure the USB drive meets the hardware requirements for Windows To Go.

Device	Drives
Imation IronKey Public USB Device	(G:)

Figure 5-13. The Windows To Go Creator

It's not a simple process to get System Center and an application portal up and running, though, so you won't want to do that unless you have good reason to. Use this option only if you want to let users self-provision their own Windows To Go drives and you have additional uses for it.

Summary

After all of the planning, considerations, and purchasing to get to a place to create Windows To Go drives, you can then choose exactly how you want to do it. You can use existing technologies and infrastructures already in place to leverage what you already own and use. You can use basic Windows images and provision drives using PowerShell. You can even use something like System Center Configuration Manager to allow users to self-provision their own drives. In Chapter 6 you'll learn how to secure the Windows To Go drives you create.

CHAPTER 6

Secure and Protect Windows To Go Drives

You've learned a lot thus far about creating and deploying Windows To Go drives, and you've learned about using BitLocker, but I haven't talked at length about any other security-related topics. In this chapter that's what I'll cover. Although some of this will be highly technical, it's important to understand the underlying technologies that go into protecting and securing data. You need to be aware of what's available and how those technologies can be used in your network to protect users' data and transmissions, and you need to have at least a basic understanding of the options available.

Because one part of securing and protecting Windows To Go drives deals with protecting the data that is created by users who employ those drives, I'll start off the chapter with additional options for managing the data users create, and data you'd like them to have access to. You'll learn about some storage options and server roles you can add to assist. Following that, I'll cover more about BitLocker, including how to manage recovery keys. Additionally, there are a few more technical items to discuss, such as combining DirectAccess with Domain Join and what's required in an enterprise to use the technologies together. Finally, I'll address the various VPN protocols and what those protocols provide in the way of secure, VPN connectivity for your Windows To Go clients.

Note Remember that one of the biggest concerns for businesses is when users bring their own devices to work. Make sure to address any issues that are likely to arise in your organization preemptively.

File and Storage Options and Services

You know not to save data to a Windows To Go drive and you know to encourage others not to either. Data should always be saved off the drive, preferably to a domain server, perhaps using a technique like folder redirection or offline files, or using a cloud option like OneDrive, a hosted SharePoint site, or even GoogleDrive. I discussed these few of these options in earlier chapters. Here I'd like to discuss some additional file and storage options and introduce you to some terms you might see as you continue to work with Windows To Go in an enterprise environment.

© Joli Ballew 2016
J. Ballew, *Windows To Go*, DOI 10.1007/978-1-4842-2134-1_6

Microsoft Azure

Microsoft Azure is a cloud computing platform and cloud infrastructure that enables enterprises to build their own applications and configure and manage their own services in the cloud, using a worldwide group of secure, managed, datacenters. Because we are concerned mostly with Windows To Go clients, Microsoft Azure might provide enterprises another solution for storing data in the cloud.

Of course, with any cloud option, security is one of the most important things to consider. In that vein it's important to note that Microsoft Azure incorporates redundant and numerous safeguards to protect your enterprise data. The technologies used to do this continue to evolve too, and you can be sure that any improvements will be implemented where applicable.

The security practices and technologies available with Microsoft Azure include:

- Azure Active Directory — Active Directory in the cloud ensures that only users who are fully authenticated and authorized can access data stored in Azure datacenters. Microsoft Azure offers multifactor authentication as well, to further protect sensitive enterprise data.

- Encryption — Microsoft Azure uses encryption to protect data as it moves among devices and datacenters. This encryption uses industry-standard protocols over all types of connections. You'll learn more about protocols later in the chapter, when we talk about securing VPNs.

- Secure Networks — Microsoft Azure uses only trusted networks and proven protocols to provide secure networks for data transmissions. The technology behind it is built on trusted security practices. The protocols ensure that the traffic you want to pass gets passed, and the traffic you don't want is blocked.

- Virtual Networks — Microsoft Azure uses virtual networks to connect your enterprise network to the datacenters to extend your on-premises network effectively and easily. You'll learn more about how virtual networks are secured toward the end of this chapter.

- Microsoft Antimalware — This software protects virtual machines as well as all Azure services. It protects against all kinds of threats, both internal and external, including viruses, worms, Trojan horses, denial-of-service attacks, and more.

In addition, you have control over your enterprise data. You control who sees what, and who can access what data. It's also important to note that Microsoft engineers do not access your data. Engineers do have access to manage the data, but only when necessary, and during the management processes they never actually look at your data. The same is true of the subcontractors they employ. Likewise, when a government entity requests access to stored data in hosted datacenters, Microsoft limits what it discloses. There is no direct access given to any government agency, and any and all requests are redirected to the customer.

To try Microsoft Azure, visit the web page shown in Figure 6-1. You can review videos and set up a free account and get a 30-day free trial. At the time this book was written, you could also get a $200 credit to spend on Azure services, allowing you to try out the entire enterprise solution for free.

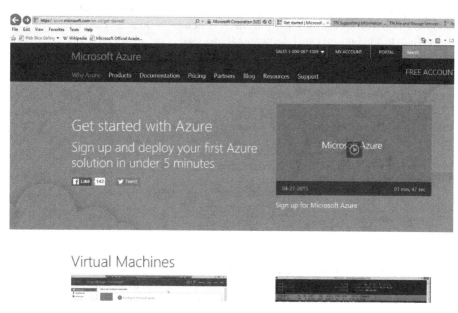

Figure 6-1. *Get a free trial account to explore Microsoft Azure*

File and Storage Services

Windows servers can be configured to serve in various capacities. You might already have a print server, data server, e-mail server, and so on in your network. With regard to Windows To Go clients, it can be useful to create a file and storage server as well. A file and storage server provides a central location where you can store users' data securely, back it up on your own terms, and manage data access. You can also put data there you'd like your users to access, such as company handbooks, forms, and so on.

To turn a Windows server into a file and storage server you'll incorporate the File and Storage Services role (it's installed by default) and then install the appropriate role services. Some specific applications you can consider when planning a file and storage server are outlined next.

Work Folders

Work Folders is a new feature only recently made available in Windows Server 2012 R2. Work Folders lets users store and access their work files on their own devices, as well as on corporate computers, for the purpose of allowing users to work from virtually

91

anywhere and from almost any type of device, even when they are offline. Their files are stored on network file servers, which are managed by network administrators, so they are secure and protected just like all other enterprise data. Like other technologies, it's possible to specify device policies (such as requiring encryption) for those users you allow to access the server and incorporate work folders on their own machines.

If you put Work Folders into place in your enterprise, and if it's not enabled on your Windows To Go workspaces during deployment, Windows To Go users can enable Work Folders from inside Control Panel. Figure 6-2 shows this.

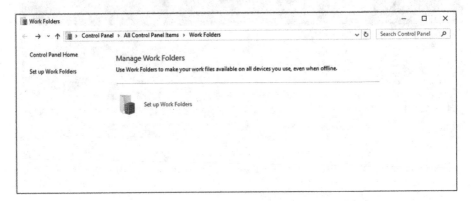

Figure 6-2. *Windows users can enable Work Folders from Control Panel*

As far as the end user goes, Work Folders should stay up to date automatically, provided it has online access for syncing when necessary. However, users can sync manually in the Work Folders window by clicking Work Folders and Sync Now.

Data Deduplication

Another server feature to consider is Data Deduplication. You might know that data is stored in blocks. Blocks are provided by hard drives and similar hardware, and you only have a limited amount of blocks to work with, no matter the scenario. Data Deduplication can help reduce the disk space requirements of the files you need to manage by reducing the number of duplicate blocks of data you store.

By incorporating Data Deduplication into your enterprise, you can save space on file storage, which, in turn, can save you money. In general terms you can reduce storage needs by half.

■ **Note** There is redundancy built in to data deduplication technologies using checksums and similar algorithms to protect data that has been modified to reduce the storage required.

---

iSCSI Target Server

iSCSI Target Server is another server role to consider because you can use it to manage storage much better than you can with other, existing technologies. Enterprises add this role to create consolidated, software-based, and iSCSI disk subsystems that they use in large storage area networks (SANs). Combined with other technologies and by also incorporating differencing virtual hard disks, enterprises can save up to 90 percent of the storage space necessary to hold the images they use for desktops, laptops, and Windows To Go drives. If you're planning on very large deployments of identical Windows To Go drives, desktops, or even servers, it's something to consider.

In addition, for applications that require raw storage that can be accessed remotely, the iSCSI Target Server role can provide continuously available block storage to those applications that need it (like Hyper-V). iSCSI Target Server also supports iSCSI on operating systems other than Windows, so you can incorporate other operating systems and devices where applicable.

Storage Spaces

Storage Spaces is another option for managing storage that's available in various Windows editions. Storage Spaces lets you group any spare disks you have and aren't using or disks you've purchased (perhaps inexpensively just for this purpose) into pools of virtual hard disks. Storage spaces that you create are scalable, which means you can add disks as more storage is needed.

Once you've created a storage space, you manage the pooled disks as one virtual disk, which makes management of these disks easier than managing multiple disks separately. If you'd like to experiment with storage pools and don't have an edition of Windows Server available to you, you can configure Storage Spaces in Windows 10. Figure 6-3 shows the applicable window in Control Panel.

Figure 6-3. *Storage Spaces is available in Windows 10*

Unified Remote Management

Prior to Windows Server 2012, if you needed to manage multiple file servers you had to incorporate Remote Desktop to connect to each server, or you had to open various instances of the applicable administration console for every computer you needed to manage. In Windows Server 2012, things changed, and it became possible to use Server Manager to perform a lot of everyday administrative functions from a single console, reducing the need to use these older methods of management. The technology that was added is Unified Remote Management.

You use Unified Remote Management on a Windows server that runs File and Storage Services. Unified management lets you perform tasks on remote servers such as restarting servers, launching administrative tools, and managing storage pools, as well as managing single volumes and even scanning for errors. You can even configure Data Deduplication and manage network shares. You can also create new iSCSI virtual disks and work with existing iSCSI virtual disks. In addition, Server Manager's Tools menu offers access to even more options, including but not limited to File Server Resource Manager, DFS Management, and Services for Network File System (NFS).

Windows PowerShell

If you haven't explored Windows PowerShell as an option to manage and protect data and network shares, it's time to do so. You can use PowerShell to automate many tasks by creating or using existing PowerShell scripts. You can use PowerShell to manage these items and more:

- Branch Cache

- Data Deduplication

- File Server Resource Manager

- iSCSI Target

- Server for NFS

- Storage

- Storage Spaces

- Work Folders

You can learn how to script with PowerShell from Microsoft's TechNet site, as well as other places. You can also open a PowerShell window from Windows 10 and type Help to learn more inside the shell itself. See Figure 6-4.

▨ Windows PowerShell

```
TOPIC
    Windows PowerShell Help System

SHORT DESCRIPTION
    Displays help about Windows PowerShell cmdlets and concepts.

LONG DESCRIPTION
    Windows PowerShell Help describes Windows PowerShell cmdlets,
    functions, scripts, and modules, and explains concepts, including
    the elements of the Windows PowerShell language.

    Windows PowerShell does not include help files, but you can read the
    help topics online, or use the Update-Help cmdlet to download help files
    to your computer and then use the Get-Help cmdlet to display the help
    topics at the command line.

    You can also use the Update-Help cmdlet to download updated help files
    as they are released so that your local help content is never obsolete.

    Without help files, Get-Help displays auto-generated help for cmdlets,
    functions, and scripts.


    ONLINE HELP
    You can find help for Windows PowerShell online in the TechNet Library
    beginning at http://go.microsoft.com/fwlink/?LinkID=108518.

    To open online help for any cmdlet or function, type:

        Get-Help <cmdlet-name> -Online

    UPDATE-HELP
    To download and install help files on your computer:

        1. Start Windows PowerShell with the "Run as administrator" option.
        2. Type:

            Update-Help

    After the help files are installed, you can use the Get-Help cmdlet to
    display the help topics. You can also use the Update-Help cmdlet to
    download updated help files so that your local help files are always
    up-to-date.

    For more information about the Update-Help cmdlet, type:

        Get-Help Update-Help -Online
-- More  --
```

Figure 6-4. Learn more about PowerShell

BitLocker in More Technical Terms

You know that BitLocker uses encryption to protect the system files stored on operating system drives, and that BitLocker protects computer hard drives from being accessed if they are removed from one computer and connected to another. It does this by checking the integrity of the system files prior to offering the logon screen. You know further that BitLocker can be used on Windows To Go drives, providing additional protection there if the drive is lost or stolen. And while I've talked a lot about why to use BitLocker and how to enable BitLocker already in this book, I've yet to discuss how BitLocker works with a TPM, how to store BitLocker keys, and the various other ways you can work with BitLocker in an enterprise.

BitLocker and TPM

BitLocker performs best and offers the most protection to the user and device when it's used on a desktop or laptop PC that is also installed with a TPM, a physical chip that is contained on the motherboard. This chip, in conjunction with BitLocker, ensures the computer and the hard drive haven't been compromised since last use. There is no access to the hard drive or logon screen until this is verified.

With a TPM, BitLocker provides the following:

- Protects against boot sector viruses as well as rootkits by ensuring that no modifications have been made to the boot files since the last check (boot). If a breach is found, BitLocker won't allow access to the drive.

- Lessens the likelihood of software attacks. Rogue software won't have access to the decryption keys it needs to access the operating system.

On computers and devices that don't include a TPM, BitLocker can still encrypt the drive and provide protection if there is some other kind of additional verification included. For a computer user, additional authentication often means inserting a USB startup key smart card, or a similar mechanism. Additionally, without a TPM, BitLocker can't provide any system integrity verifications as it would on a computer with one. It is the TPM that provides this verification, so it makes sense that can't happen if a TPM doesn't exist.

If a USB startup key, smart card, or similar device won't work as a security mechanism, such as is the case with a removable drive, the user can input a PIN. Windows To Go workspaces use a PIN.

Note that a computer with a TPM must also have a compatible BIOS that can communicate with the TPM and startup system. What's required is a Trusted Computing Group (TCG)-compliant BIOS. Computers that come with a TPM will likely come with the required BIOS; I've never heard of an instance where it doesn't, at least not with computers from major manufacturers. For all computer systems, the BIOS must support the USB mass storage device class.

BitLocker and Recovery Keys

When you enable BitLocker on a Windows To Go drive, the BitLocker process creates a recovery key. The recovery key, sometimes called a recovery password, is a 48-digit, randomly generated number. If you ever need to access a drive that is BitLocker enabled and you don't know the PIN or password, or have access to any other mechanism to unlock that drive, you'll need to have that key handy to recover the drive. Thus, having a plan to store the recovery keys for your users is extremely important.

There are lots of ways to store the key, including writing it down, storing it to a cloud drive, storing it on a domain server, and more. You could even save it to the Windows To Go drive, although that would not be any help if the drive wasn't accessible.

If you haven't backed up your key, from your Windows To Go drive, access the option to back up an existing recovery key from the BitLocker area of Control Panel. Figure 6-5 shows this option.

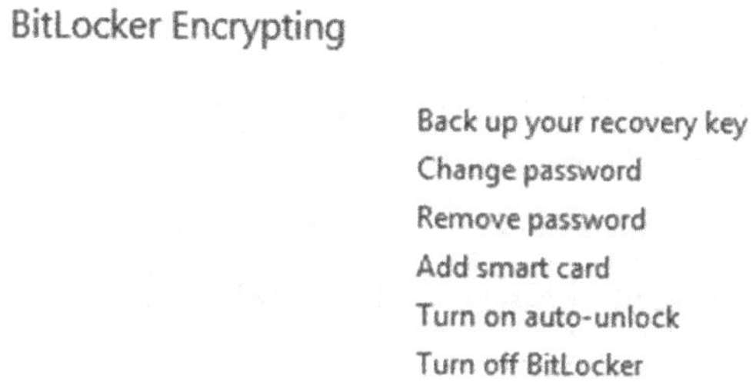

BitLocker Encrypting

Back up your recovery key

Change password

Remove password

Add smart card

Turn on auto-unlock

Turn off BitLocker

Figure 6-5. You can back up a recovery key from Control Panel

In an enterprise, backing up recovery keys isn't left to the end user. Instead, a Group Policy setting is configured to automatically back up those keys to an Active Directory domain server. You can review the Group Policy Setting on a Windows 10 computer by following these steps:

1. Log on to the computer as an administrator.

2. Use the Windows key + R combination to open a Run dialog box.

3. Type gpedit.msc and click OK.

4. Navigate to **Computer Configuration\Administrative Templates\Windows Components**.

5. Click BitLocker Drive Encryption.

6. Double-click Store BitLocker recovery information in Active Directory Domain Services (Windows Server 2008 and Windows Vista).

7. Note the setting is enabled by default.

8. Close all dialog boxes and windows.

How BitLocker Works

You know BitLocker can be configured for use with a TPM to protect a drive. In a device with a TPM, the encryption keys are locked until the TPM verifies system integrity. This works as follows:

1. During startup, the TPM compares a hash it has already collected during the last successful computing session with the one that exists now.

2. The two values are compared.

3. If the values are the same, the TPM releases the decryption key. If the values do not agree, no key is offered and the boot process stops.

4. If TPM is combined with another authentication requirement, like a PIN, that must be input before boot-up continues.

If there's no TPM, the user is required to input the proper credentials to unlock the encryption key and thus enable access to the drive.

Secure Access Between the Host and a Windows To Go Workspace

If you've ever used Windows To Go and tried to access the host's internal hard drives, you know that you can't (or you're not supposed to be able to). This is part of the built-in security that comes with Windows To Go. The same is true of the host. If the host is running and a Windows To Go drive is inserted, that drive should not be accessible either. But this isn't always the case; with the right knowledge and a few clicks of the mouse, a host can access a Windows To Go drive.

Because it is possible to access a Windows To Go drive from a host if you are really tech-savvy, it's best to use the NoDefaultDriveLetter attribute when provisioning the USB drive. If the user does know how to assign a drive letter, the drive will display in Windows Explorer once it's mounted. The attribute you need to apply is applied automatically if you create the drive using the Windows To Go creator.

With the proper security mechanisms in place, when a Windows To Go drive is inserted into a running host, the host will not be able to see the Windows To Go drive but will still be able to see other drives attached as applicable. Figure 6-6 shows a computer with various drives and partitions, but notice that you can't see the attached Windows To Go drive.

Figure 6-6. *The host can access all of its attached drives and partitions but can't, by default, see an attached Windows To Go drive.*

Now, if you are the host and have a Windows To Go drive attached and you need to access the contents of that drive, you can mount the drive in the Disk Management Console and then access that data from File Explorer.

To mount a Windows To Go drive using the Disk Management Console:

1. Use Windows key + R to open a Run dialog box.

2. Type diskmgmt.msc and click OK.

3. In Disk Management, right-click the drive (it might be in the Disk 2 section) and select Change Drive Letter and Path.

4. In the resulting dialog box, shown in Figure 6-7, click Add, and select a drive letter.

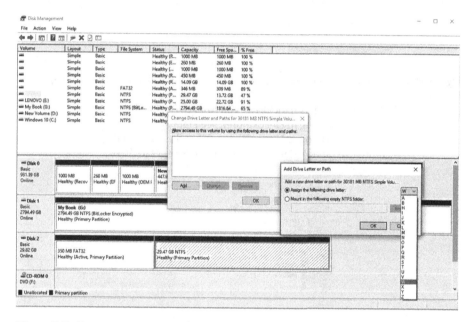

Figure 6-7. *You can mount a Windows To Go drive in Disk Management to enable access to its contents*

5. Note that the drive letter is assigned; open File Explorer to see the mounted drive. See Figure 6-8 (as compared to Figure 6-6).

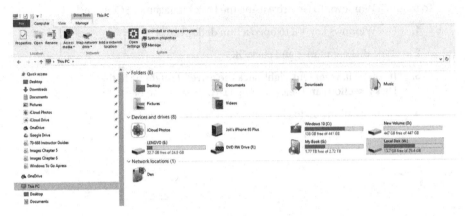

Figure 6-8. *Once you've mounted the Windows To Go drive you can access it from File Explorer*

6. Finally, note what's on the drive. You can access the files on it by double-clicking in File Explorer. See Figure 6-9. (Here I've drilled down to the User's files, and into the Joli Ballew account. I've input administrator credentials to get to these personal files.)

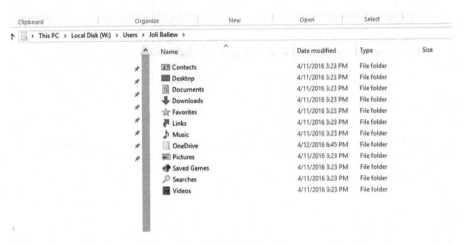

Figure 6-9. *A host can access a Windows To Go drive if it's been mounted in Disk Management*

7. To remove the drive letter, repeat the process above, only click Remove in Step 4.

■ **Caution**   Know that without the proper safeguards in place, an unattended Windows To Go drive might be accessible if the host's user is tech-savvy and knows how to mount a drive in Disk Management.

DirectAccess and Domain Join

I've mentioned both DirectAccess and Domain Join in this book but I'd like to go into a little more depth here. DirectAccess is an additional role service of the Remote Access server role and it enables users to access the network and the resources on it without using a VPN connection. With this technology, clients are always connected to the enterprise, provided they're online. This isn't a solution where users need to start a connection or stop one. If a client is running and Internet-connected, the client is connected to your enterprise.

DirectAccess is a pretty new technology, though, and isn't supported on all clients. This list shows what editions of Windows can use DirectAccess as either a server or a client:

- All versions of Windows Server 2012 R2

- All versions of Windows Server 2012

- All versions of Windows Server 2008 R2

This list shows what editions of Windows clients support DirectAccess:

- Windows 10 Enterprise

- Windows 10 Enterprise 2015 Long Term Servicing Branch (LTSB)

- Windows 8 Enterprise

- Windows 7 Ultimate

- Windows 7 Enterprise

Domain Join was introduced in Windows Server 2008 R2. This feature lets computers join a domain without ever actually contacting a domain controller. You can perform this task during the provisioning process and join computers or Windows To Go drives to the domain immediately after installation completes, to make the provisioning and deployment process for efficient.

■ **Note**   When Domain Join is used it establishes a trust relationship between a compatible Windows computer or Windows To Go drive and an Active Directory domain.

Offline Domain Join is an extension of Domain Join and can provide the following enhancements to your network infrastructure:

- When large numbers of computers or drives are provisioned, during a normal Domain Join process the computer would need to be rebooted. With Offline Domain Join you can input the Domain Join information on the production computer, and make it part of the deployment and provisioning process. Done this way, no additional restart is required.

- When you use Domain Join with a read-only domain controller you reduce the number of steps previously required to complete the process.

- If you use deployment tools such as Windows System Image Manager, you can perform an unattended Domain Join. You provide the information in your Unattend.xml file. Again, doing so saves both time and resources.

Once you've decided to use Domain Join, you use the command-line utility Djoin.exe to get started. The general steps for using Djoin.exe are:

1. Run **djoin /provision**. This creates the computer account metadata.

2. Note the resulting text file.

3. Run **djoin /requestODJ**. Insert the computer account metadata from the .txt file into the Windows directory of the destination computer.

4. Reboot the destination computer.

5. Wait while the computer joins the domain.

For more information on DirectAccess and Domain Join, refer to the articles available at Microsoft TechNet's site.

Securing Data Transmissions via VPN

VPNs are networks that provide connections that are used to join two computers across a private or public network, such as the Internet. VPNs use a variety of TCP/IP tunneling protocols to secure these connections.

So how does this work? To start, the VPN client works within the protocol parameters to call to and connect to a virtual port on a VPN server, which ultimately authenticates the caller and allows access to the network. In many of our scenarios in this book, a Windows To Go client would use a VPN to connect to a Windows-based virtual server on an enterprise network, for the purpose of gaining access to network resources, storing and accessing data, and so on.

To secure connections, a virtual point-to-point link is established between the client and server. Data that is sent is encapsulated and encrypted for security. The encapsulation includes information, in the form of a header, about where the data comes from and where it's going, among other things. The data also incorporates encryption information, including encryption keys. If the data is breached on its way to the destination, it won't be readable. Only a computer with the proper decryption keys can unencrypt the data.

There are two types of VPNs. One is a VPN connection where users who are away from the office access network resources over the Internet. This is a remote access VPN and is what your Windows To Go users will employ. The other is a connection where two routers are involved instead of a client and a server. The two routers often connect separate facilities in the same organization, or two organizations that form a trust. When routers are connected, data packets are forwarded from one to the other and back.

VPNS AREN'T RIGHT FOR EVERY ENVIRONMENT

Here are a few reasons why you would not opt for a VPN:

- If the organization is using an Internet-based VPN, reliability and performance will be not under the business's direct control.

- Despite what it sounds like in the real world a VPN isn't particularly easy for a business to create or deploy since a lot of cases and scenarios must be considered.

- VPNs can pose a security risk when used with wireless devices.

VPN Protocols

VPN protocols are often referred to as tunneling protocols. Tunneling is what enables the encapsulation of packets, and it is also what secures them. Tunneling technologies are what allows for data to be transmitted over and through different types of networks too, such as data that comes from a private enterprise to and through the Internet to another private enterprise or client.

A protocol is a set of rules and standards that allows systems to communicate effectively. Computers use protocols to define how transmissions occur and under what circumstances. The protocol used depends on what's required of the transmission. It also depends on the client. Because protocols evolve over time, a computer running Windows XP doesn't always support all of the protocols that a computer running Windows 10 will. The same is true of servers. A Windows 2000 Server has far fewer capabilities than, say, a Server 2008 R2 or a Server 2012 computer does, and this includes protocol support.

In the upcoming sections I'll introduce you to some common protocols including PPTP, L2TP, and SSTP. If you'd like to see how to configure a specific protocol prior to reviewing the options you can do so by creating a VPN on an applicable client machine and then looking at the properties for that connection. Here's how to do that on a

Windows To Go drive running Windows 10, and note that you don't actually have to have network credentials, you can create an imaginary VPN you'll never use:

1. Right-click the network icon on the Taskbar and click Open Network and Sharing Center.

2. Click Set up a new connection or network.

3. Choose Connect to a workplace and click Next. See Figure 6-10.

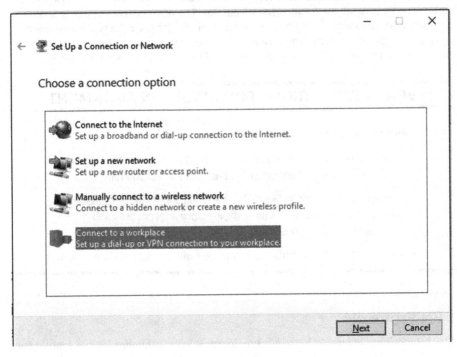

Figure 6-10. Set up a VPN by creating connection to a workplace

4. Click Use My Internet Connection (VPN).

5. Type Contoso.com for the VPN name. Change the Destination name if desired. See Figure 6-11.

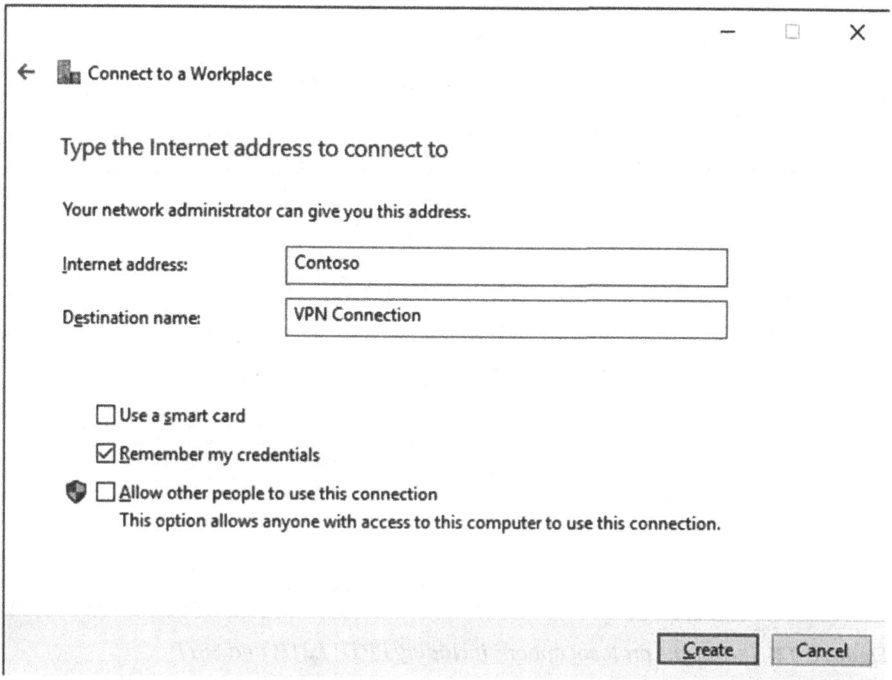

Figure 6-11. Complete the process for creating a VPN

6. Leave the default settings and click Create.

7. Back at the Network and Sharing Center, on the left side click Change Adapter Settings.

8. Right-click the new VPN and click Properties.

9. In the VPN Connections Properties dialog box, click the Security tab.

10. Click the arrow under Type of VPN, shown in Figure 6-12.
    Note the protocol options.

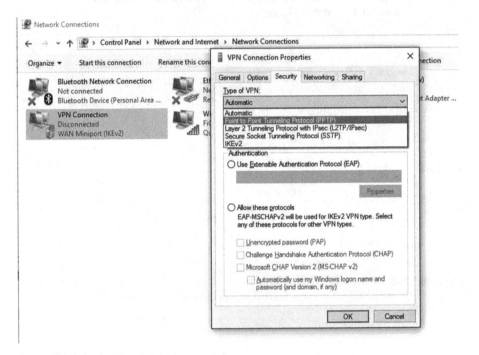

Figure 6-12. Locate the protocol options including PPTP, L2TP, and SSTP

11. Click Cancel and close all open windows.

Now that you've seen where to configure protocols for VPN connections, let's take a closer look at what these protocols offer. You can use all three for VPN connections too. However, they do have differences.

PPTP

You'll use this protocol to send multiprotocol traffic across a private IP intranet network or a public one, like the Internet. When data transmissions occur over the Internet, the VPN server incorporates two network interfaces. The first connects to the Internet, the second the intranet. You can use this protocol for remote access and site-to-site VPN connections too.

■ **Caution** Note that PPTP has its own set of risks because the protocol is no longer secure, as cracking the initial MS-CHAPv2 authentication can be reduced to the difficulty of cracking a single DES (Data Encryption Standard) 56-bit key.

The encapsulation process uses IP datagrams for transmission and encapsulates PPP frames. These frames can be encrypted or compressed, or both encrypted and compressed. The PPP frame uses Microsoft Point-to-Point Encryption (MPPE). Encryption keys are created from either the MS-CHAP v2 or EAP-TLS authentication process. MS-CHAP v2 is user-level authentication. This prevents unauthorized users from calling the router. EAP-TLS is a more secure than MS-CHAP v2. It's also user-level authentication and can be used on a dial-up, PPTP VPN, or L2TP/IPSec VPN connection. EAP-TLS requires the enterprise have a certificate infrastructure, because it requires a user certificate to call the router. It also requires a computer certificate for the server performing the authentication.

Virtual private networking clients like those who use Windows To Go must use the MS-CHAP v2 or EAP-TLS authentication protocol if they need their PPP frames to be encrypted. PPTP-based VPN connections do not provide data integrity though. Data integrity is what verifies that the data wasn't tampered with during the transmission process, but it doesn't verify that data was sent by a user who had been previously been authorized.

PPTP can be used with Microsoft Windows 2000, Windows XP, Windows Vista, Windows 7, 8, and 8.1, and Windows 10 as well as all editions of Windows Server 2008 and 2012. PPTP does not require the use of a public key infrastructure (PKI), which enterprises would need to incorporate if they wanted to create, and manage, use and store, and revoke digital certificates, among other things.

L2TP

You'll use this protocol to send encrypted, multiprotocol traffic over any type of network, provided it supports point-to-point delivery. L2TP provides IPSec encryption and encapsulation. The combination of L2TP and IPsec is referred to as L2TP/IPsec. There are some concerns here as well, though, such as getting around firewalls. Use L2TP over PPTP though, when more secure protocols can't be implemented.

To use this protocol both the VPN client and server have to support it. Almost all Windows computers in use today do and L2TP is installed by default with the TCP/IP protocol. Support is built in Windows XP and Vista clients, as well as those after. Any server that's Windows Server 2003 and beyond is supported too.

With L2TP, data packets are encapsulated with two layers of protection. The PPP datagram is wrapped with appropriate header information and wrapped again with an IPSec header and trailer. The entire message is encrypted with either DES or Triple DES (3DES). The Internet Key Exchange (IKE) is used to generate the encryption keys.

With this protocol some sort of authentication method is required. These can be computer certificates (recommended) or preshared keys. If you opt for certificates you'll need access to a PKI to issue them. The protocol when used correctly provides more protection than PPTP because it provides data integrity and confidentiality, among other things. Like PPTP, L2TP can be used with clients running Windows 2000, Windows XP, or Windows Vista, as well as Windows 7, 8, 8.1, and 10. Windows Server 2003 and later are compatible too.

SSTP

This is a newer protocol than the previous two, and it encapsulates PPP datagrams through the SSL protocol and uses certificates to verify identities. It uses the HTTPS protocol over TCP port 443 to transfer the data. It can pass data through firewalls that might otherwise block the previously discussed protocols.

Data is encapsulated with PPP over the Secure Sockets Layer (SSL) channel of the HTTPS protocol. Thus it's possible to incorporate better security, key negotiation, and encryption because it supports authentication protocols like EAP-TLS.

Because SSTP is a newer protocol, it can only be used with client computers running Windows Vista Service Pack 1 (SP1) and higher or Windows Server 2008 and higher. Like L2TP with IPSec, this protocol provides data integrity, data confidentiality, and data authentication.

Summary of VPN Connections

VPN connections that use any of the three protocols outlined here provide some form of encapsulation, encryption, and authentication of data and transmissions. Encapsulation wraps the datagrams with a header that contains routing information. The information added depends on the protocol selected.

The data is encrypted by the sending computer and decrypted by the receiving computer. Encrypting and decryption depend on shared encryption keys. Both the sender and receiver must recognize and have the required keys to complete the transmission. Because data is encrypted with keys, anyone who intercepts packets can't read them without the proper decryption key.

Authentication can be user-level authentication, where the VPN server authenticates the client using PPP, or it can be computer-level authentication, where IPSec is used in combination with preshared keys or computer certificates. The latter type of connection is available with L2TP/IPSec communication.

Summary

It's important to understand the available security mechanisms and protocols used to protect Windows To Go drives, so that you can make educated decisions during planning processes. Once those decisions are made, it's important to know how you'll manage the data your Windows To Go users create while on their drives. There are many options for that, including in house, in the cloud, or hybrid solutions. In Chapter 7 you'll learn about using Windows 10 in a business scenario, focusing on your end users and practical applications.

CHAPTER 7

■ ■ ■

Windows 10 for Business

It's likely that your employees have been using Windows 8/8.1, or possibly even Windows 7, prior to your giving them a Windows To Go workspace running Windows 10. If that's the case, you'll need to provide some training on how to use the new operating system prior to sending them out into the field with it. In this chapter I'll outline what they need to know to get on board with Windows 10 as quickly as possible.

To get you started, I'll address the newer features first, for those employees who are familiar with Windows 8/8.1, including how to use the new Start menu, the Store (if it's enabled), Cortana, the Microsoft Edge web browser, and Virtual Desktops. I'll introduce you to Settings, a new, unified place to configure how you want Windows to behave and perform. After that I'll address how to work with various networks, how to connect, how to modify network adapter settings, and so on. I'll address local accounts, Microsoft accounts, and domain accounts too, so that all possible usages for Windows To Go get some screen time here. I'll talk about File Explorer too, and how users incorporate OneDrive, Google Drive, and so on, for those users who don't belong to a domain and need some way to save files off the drive.

The Start Menu

Windows 10 has a new Start menu. Part of this and the reasoning behind creating Windows 10 the way Microsoft did was to try to unify the various software platforms across all of the available Windows devices. So, this Start menu replaces the Start screen introduced in Windows 8/8.1 and gives users a more familiar look and feel no matter what device they are on. There's a Start button in the bottom left corner that users can click to get to familiar places like Control Panel, the Documents folder, Network settings and so on. Users can right-click the Start button to access a sort of "power" menu which includes links to the Command prompt and Device Manager, among other things. The Start menu also offers access to the installed apps, like Mail and Maps. Figure 7-1 shows what my Start menu looks like. Note that you can configure the menu to look just about any way you like.

© Joli Ballew 2016
J. Ballew, *Windows To Go*, DOI 10.1007/978-1-4842-2134-1_7

Figure 7-1. *The Windows Start menu looks quite a bit different from what users are likely familiar with, and offers two panels side by side, with the left column showing pinned items, recently added items, and most used apps*

You can also see in Figure 7-1 that there's an option to search directly from the Taskbar. This is how your users will likely opt to find things like files, folders, applications, and settings. You can type anything there, and the results generally offer what you're looking for.

You can also right-click any item you see on the Start Menu or in the tiles area (that's the right side of the Start menu) to edit it. For instance, you can right-click an item in the list on the left to remove it from the list, uninstall it from the computer, or pin it to the Start menu, among other things. When you opt to pin an item to the Start menu it appears as a tile in the left pane. Figure 7-2 shows some of these options.

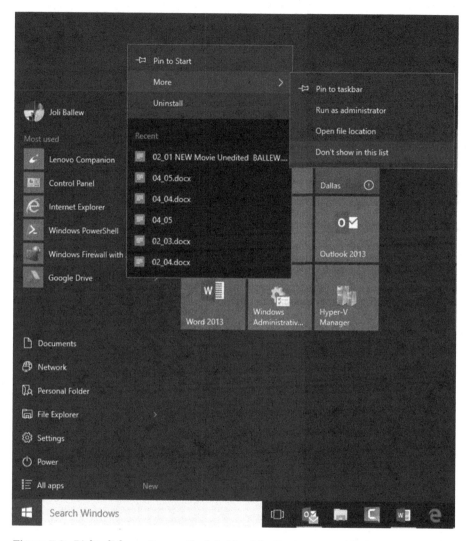

Figure 7-2. Right-click any item on the left side of the Start menu to edit it

You can edit how the Start menu looks by dragging and dropping the tiles on the right side as well. Figure 7-3 shows this in action. To do this, simply hold down the left mouse button as you drag, and once the item is where you want it, let go of that button. After you try this, right-click any tile to see options to resize, turn a live tile off (that's a tile that changes as information does, like e-mail or the weather), and more.

Figure 7-3. Drag and drop any tile to move it

Finally, at the bottom of the Start screen, on the left side, is the option All apps. Click All apps to see a list of the applications installed on your computer. If you find an app you never use, you can access the uninstall option by right-clicking. You can also pin any app to the Start screen or Taskbar among other things.

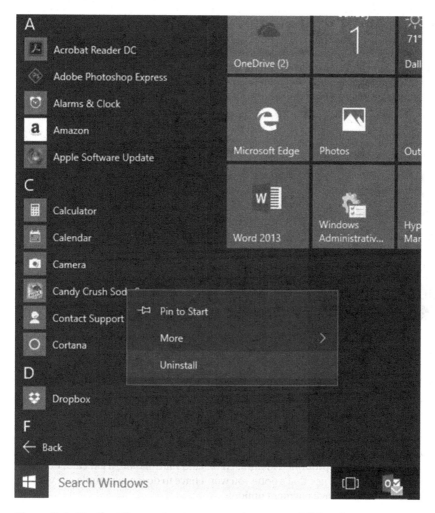

Figure 7-4. Use the All apps view to access and manage additional apps

■ **Note** Windows 8 and 8.1 offered apps that opened in their own special window in full screen mode and were not available on the desktop, nor could they be specifically resized by the user (although they could be snapped to one side or the other). Universal apps now available in Windows 10 can be used in traditional windows on the desktop.

The Microsoft Store

You may or may not have access to the Microsoft Store from your Windows To Go drive, but if you do, you can explore it now to see what's available. To access the Store, click the Start button and then the Store tile. If you don't see the tile, type Store in the Search Windows box on the Taskbar and select it from the resulting list. Figure 7-5 shows the Store.

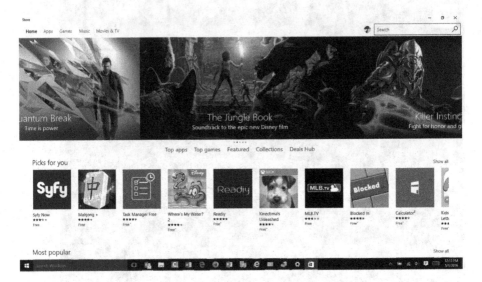

Figure 7-5. *The Store offers a place to obtain apps*

To obtain an app that is free, you simply click the app you want and click Free. The app will install and be ready to use within a few seconds. The first time you try to purchase an app, you'll be prompted to input credit card information, a gift card, or similar form of payment. Once that's done you won't have to do it again until your card expires or you want to change payment options.

Cortana

Cortana is Microsoft's digital voice assistant, which is Microsoft's voice-controlled addition to Windows. It hopes to make it easier to interact with Windows without using a keyboard or moving a mouse. You can talk to Cortana the same way you likely already talk to your phone, by asking questions, saying commands, and asking Cortana to remind you of things or tell you about the weather or traffic conditions. The first time you use Windows Search on the Taskbar you'll probably be prompted to set it up, but if you miss that or want to do it later, there is a small circle available after you click inside the Search Windows area that will let you pick up where you left off. Figure 7-6 shows this. From the screen shown here, just work through the setup process. Cortana will get to know your voice, where you live, and so on, and then you can use it effectively.

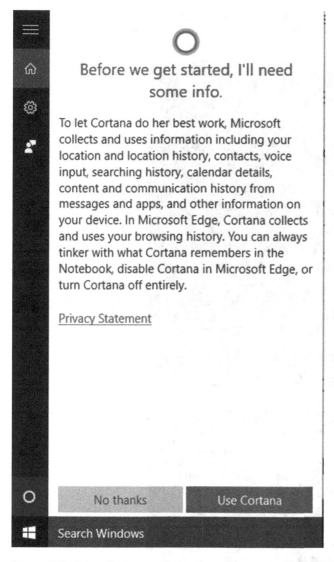

Figure 7-6. Set up Cortana so that you can incorporate the built-in digital assistant in Windows 10

To use voice commands you address Cortana using the "Hey Cortana" feature. With this on, you say "Hey Cortana," and Cortana will ask you how she can help. You need to enable this feature though, as follows:

1. Type "Cortana settings" in the Search area of the Taskbar.

2. Click Cortana and Search Settings in the results.

3. Switch the toggle from Off to On under "Cortana can give you suggestions, ideas, reminders, alerts and more." See Figure 7-7.

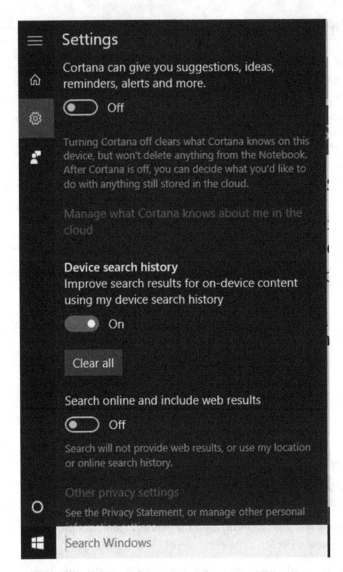

Figure 7-7. Enable Cortana to recognize your voice

■ **Note**   Windows 10 provides a new way to access all notifications from a single place. It collects alerts from all of your devices and from all installed apps and provides notifications in real time.

---

4.   Configure other options as desired.

5.   Opt to use Cortana if prompted and follow any additional setup suggestions.

Here are some commands and questions you can ask Cortana once it's up and running:

• What's the weather like?

• What's my schedule look like today?

• Is my flight on time?

• Give me directions to . . . .

• What's traffic like today?

• Hey Cortana, create an appointment.

• When is my next appointment?

• Set an alarm for . . . .

• When is Memorial Day?

• What's on TV tonight?

• What time is it in France?

• Where can I go to eat tonight?

• What's in a Long Island Ice Tea?

And so on . . . .

Remember too that Cortana can search your hard drive for specific folders and files, and can even send e-mails while you're doing something else, like working on a spreadsheet, which makes multitasking all that more efficient.

Microsoft Edge

Microsoft Edge is a new web browser available from Microsoft and included with Windows 10. There's an icon for it on the Taskbar. It has an app-like feel to it, but it's a desktop application. It's streamlined, so it's a good browser for tablet users, or those with smaller monitors. You use it as you would any web browser, and configure settings by clicking the ellipsis and clicking Settings in the results. Figure 7-8 shows this option. From Settings you can configure home pages, block pop-ups, use Adobe Flash Player, and more. As far as security goes, ActiveX is gone and the AppContainer Sandbox is always on. Flash is still enabled by default though; something to keep in mind if you're planning to use it out of the box.

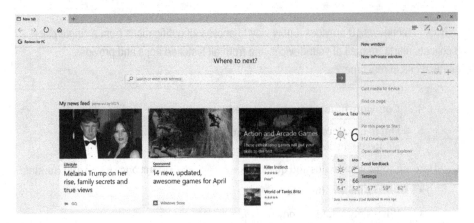

Figure 7-8. Microsoft Edge is a new web browsing experience available in Windows 10

■ **Note**   Microsoft has been working on the Spartan Project, a new web browser that will offer instant sharing, distraction-free reading, built-in PDF support, better ways to search and with more efficiency, and more ways to work than ever before.

Multitasking with Virtual Desktops

Virtual Desktops is a new feature of Windows 10 that enables users to create more than one desktop and switch among them easily. It's like having multiple versions of Windows open at the same time. The default setup is one desktop, which is what users know and use now, no matter what operating system they have experience with. But it's possible to add another desktop, and, in fact, multiple desktops.

Some users find that they enjoy Windows 10 more if they use their default desktop for things they do for work, such as open applications, spreadsheets, web browsers, documents, and so on, and keep another desktop for personal items like personal e-mail, photos, their favorite web browser, and so on. Figure 7-9 shows how to create a virtual desktop.

Figure 7-9. *Create a virtual desktop*

Here are the steps:

1. Click the Virtual Desktop icon on the Taskbar. It's next to the Search window on the Taskbar.

2. Click the + sign in the bottom right corner of the screen.

3. Click the new desktop, named Desktop 2.

4. Note that there is nothing on that desktop. Open apps and such as desired.

5. To switch to the previous desktop, click the Virtual Desktop button again, and select the desired desktop.

Once you have at least one virtual desktop configured, explore the Virtual Desktop settings. You can find those settings by searching for them in the Search window of the Taskbar. There are only two settings to configure:

- On the Taskbar, show windows that are open: Only on the desktop I'm using or All Desktops.

- Pressing Alt + Tab shows windows that are open: Only on the desktop I'm using or All Desktops.

■ **Tip** You can use Snap Assist with the virtual desktops you create just as you can when working in a single desktop. Snap Assist lets you "snap" two windows next to each other on the screen and pin up to four different apps onto one screen. Snap Assist works differently in tablet mode but should work great for Windows To Go users.

Settings

Windows 7 offered Control Panel for making configuration changes to Windows. Windows 8 and 8.1 offered that as well (as does Windows 10) but a new feature was added, called Settings. That was available from the Charms bar. In Windows 10, Settings still exists but the Charms bar is gone. You open Settings from the Start menu. This opens a Control Panel-like area where you can make changes to how your computer functions. Figure 7-10 shows the Settings window. If you don't see this screen when you open Settings, you've previously navigated away from it, so you'll need to click the Settings icon in whatever window appears, to return to this home screen for the Settings window.

Figure 7-10. *Settings offers a place to make system-wide changes in lieu of using Control Panel*

There are several sections: System, Devices, Network and Internet, Personalization, Accounts, Time and Language, Ease of Access, Privacy, and Update and Security. It's important to know what's available in each section, so I'll introduce each briefly here.

System

The System area of Settings offers a place users can personalize their system settings, at least those that aren't managed by a domain administrator through Group Policy or a local administrator using Local Group Policy. Users might want to configure how many notifications they receive from Windows with regard to, say, Microsoft OneDrive, Skype, and things like "Get Office" reminders. They can configure Power options too, at least as they are applicable to Windows To Go workspaces. They can configure their default apps as well, perhaps to make Microsoft Outlook their default e-mail application instead of the Mail app, or Internet Explorer as the default instead of Microsoft Edge.

Figure 7-11 shows the System window with Multitasking selected. Here users can decide if they want to use features such as Snap (Snap Assist was mentioned earlier in a Note), and how they want to configure the virtual desktops they create (more on this later). Like other areas of Settings, the changes they make here are saved to their user profile and are applied no matter what host they use.

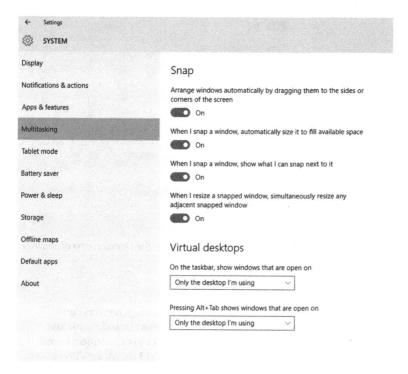

Figure 7-11. *The System window offers users a place to customize system settings*

■ **Note**   To return to the main Settings window after navigating away from it, click the wheel icon next to Settings in the top left corner of the screen, or click the Back button.

Devices

The Devices area of Settings lets users configure settings for the devices attached to their device, and in the case of Windows To Go, these devices might include attached printers, but more likely users will come here to configure things like AutoPlay and Typing settings. Figure 7-12 shows the typing settings, and as with other settings the changes made here become part of the Windows To Go user's profile.

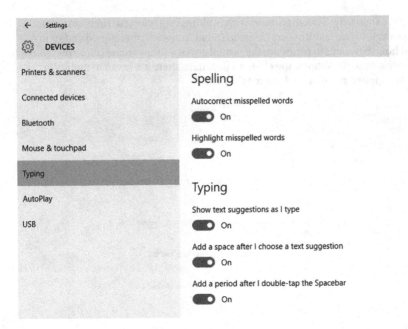

Figure 7-12. *Change settings that have to do with devices under the Devices area of Settings*

Network and Internet

Users will come to the Network and Internet area of Settings to manage networks and network settings. Here they can connect and disconnect from networks and enable and disable Airplane Mode (although they can also do that from the Taskbar), connect to and manage VPNs, and view data usage among other things. Figure 7-13 shows the VPN options.

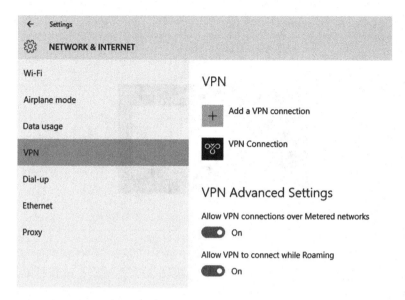

Figure 7-13. Users configure VPN settings in the Network and Internet area of Settings

Personalization

This is the area of Windows where users can configure personalization options such as desktop backgrounds and screensavers. They can configure the Lock screen too including what's shown on it, although with Windows To Go this isn't something users employ that often. Users can apply themes too, which are groupings of backgrounds, screensavers, sounds, mouse pointers, and so on. Anything you can do here you can also do in Control Panel, as is the case with most of the Settings options. Figure 7-14 shows the Personalization area of Windows 10 with Start selected. Here is where you configure the Start menu options.

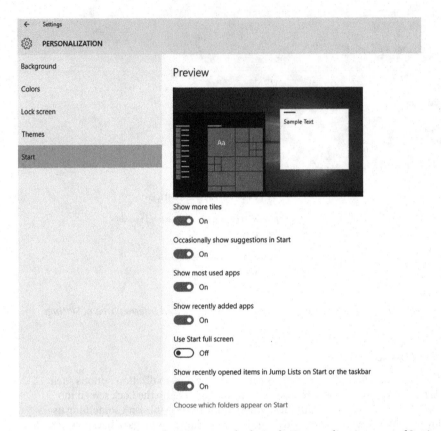

Figure 7-14. Configure how the Start menu looks in the Personalization area of Settings

Accounts

You use the Accounts area of Settings to configure user accounts, account profiles, and work access and to configure Family Settings and more. A unique feature here for Windows To Go users is the Work Access area. Here, as shown in Figure 7-15, users can:

- Sign in to Azure AD — Azure AD is the option you can guide your users to if they need to sign in to Office 365 using an existing work or school account. You might preconfigure this during the provisioning process.

- Enroll in to device management — Device Management is a feature of larger enterprises where the network administrator manages the devices user bring to work and limits what they can do with those devices while connected to the corporate network. Administrators can deploy certificates, Wi-Fi, VPN, and e-mail profiles automatically using this technology and allow users to access corporate resources with the appropriate security configurations.

- Join or leave an organization — Clicking this feature opens the About page in System Settings, allowing a user to leave an organization, join an Azure domain, and so on.

- Add or remove a management package — Used to manage the packages installed on the Windows To Go drive, specifically those used with Device Management features.

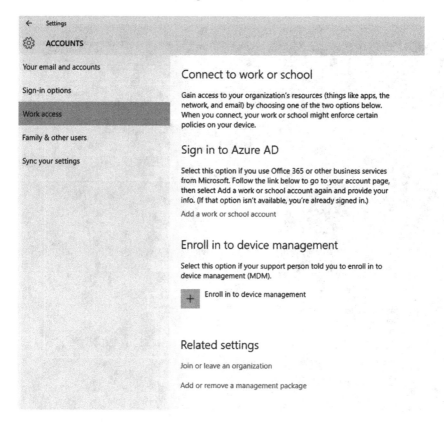

Figure 7-15. *Use the Work Access area of Accounts, in Settings to configure access to work-related resources*

Time and Language

Here is where users can change, as applicable to them as allowed by Group Policy, settings related to time and language. You can change the time zone here, as well as date and time formats. Changes to language and country can be defined here too, and you can configure speech recognition settings.

Ease of Access

From Ease of Access users can configure, enable, and use features like Magnifier and Narrator, configure high contrast, and make other system changes that make it easier for people with disabilities to use Windows To Go. There are options for Closed Captioning, Keyboard, and Mouse as well. Figure 7-16 shows the setting High Contrast #1, which I've applied, which can be enabled for users who have trouble viewing the computer screen.

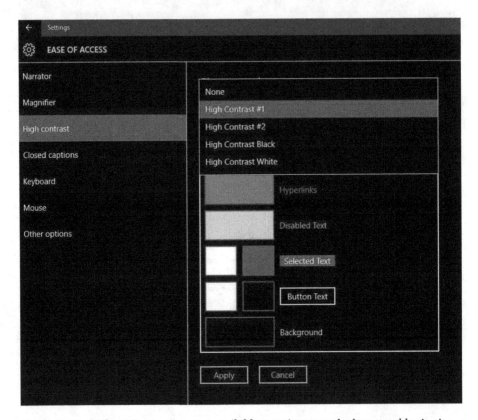

Figure 7-16. *High contrast settings are available to assist users who have trouble viewing the screen*

Privacy

The Privacy settings offer more options than any other area of settings. As you can see in Figure 7-17, there are lots of ways to configure privacy options. One of these options is Location Services. Location Services is necessary when using Cortana, as well as apps like Maps and Weather. In fact, you'll be prompted to enable Location Services when you use these apps and features for the first time. You can make changes to Location Services here, including choosing what apps can have access to your location.

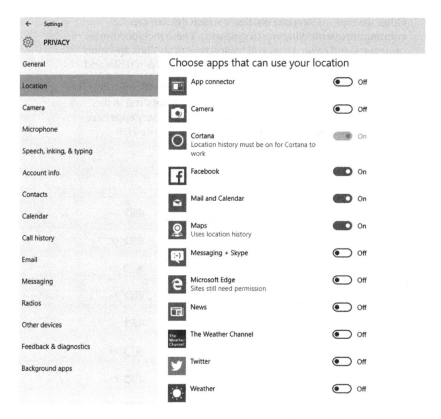

Figure 7-17. *Location Services uses your location to make your Windows Experience more useful*

Other features here that Windows To Go users might want to configure include:

- Speech, inking, & typing — Lets users allow Windows to learn their speech habits, access contacts, and even review handwriting samples to better understand how they use Windows.

- Contacts — Users can choose which apps can access their contacts list.

- Calendar — Users can choose which apps can access their calendar entries.

- Email — Users can configure which apps can access their default e-mail account to send e-mail from it.

127

- Other devices — Users can configure which devices can communicate with Windows to sync with. These include Xboxes, projectors, and so on. Users will have access to an Xbox app soon too, which will enable them to play games on a PC or a tablet and not just on an Xbox console.

- Background apps — Users can configure which apps run in the background. Users might want to turn off unnecessary apps here like Microsoft Jigsaw or Get Office, as shown in Figure 7-18.

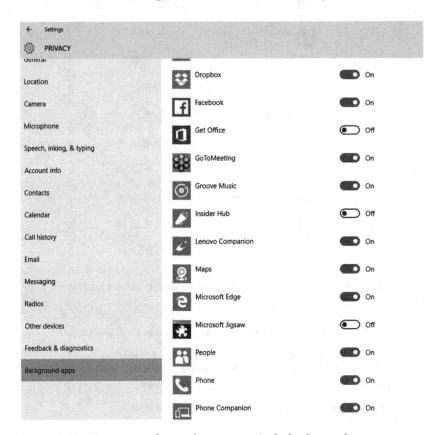

Figure 7-18. *Users can configure what apps run in the background*

Update and Security

Although users might be prohibited from making too many changes here, especially those in an enterprise, users of single Windows To Go drives will find plenty to work with. In Update & Security, shown in Figure 7-19, users can:

- Access Windows Update, check for, and install updates.

- Turn on or off Windows Defender and Cloud Protection.

- Configure File History, Windows 10 backup program.

- Activate Windows.

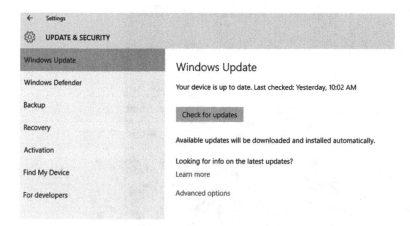

Figure 7-19. *Users can protect their Windows To Go drives from Update & Security*

■ **Note** Although Recovery is an option here, Windows To Go drives can't be recovered. They must be reprovisioned.

Networks

Windows To Go users will connect to lots of networks over the life of the workspace. In fact, they'll connect to a network virtually every time they use the drive. It's important to teach users the ways they can access network settings and how to use those settings not only to connect but also to troubleshoot when necessary.

There are three main ways users will work with networks and network settings: the Taskbar, the Network and Sharing Center, and the Network and Internet area of Settings. Let's take a closer look at some of the available options.

Taskbar Settings

There's a network icon on the Taskbar. Users might already be familiar with this from other editions of Windows. However, when you click the network icon in Windows 10, a new type of menu appears that's much different from previous versions. As you can see in Figure 7-20, all nearby networks are shown, as well as any configured VPNs. Users can click any item in this list to connect, provided they have the required credentials.

They can also disconnect from networks here. As you can see, they can also enable and disable Airplane mode.

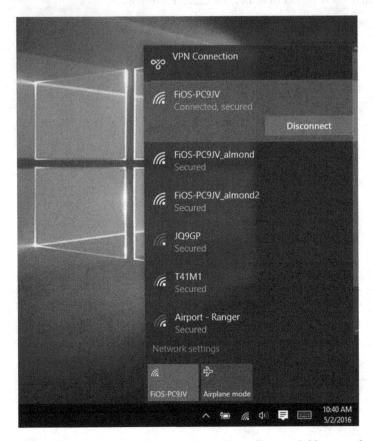

Figure 7-20. *The Network icon on the Taskbar offers available networks*

■ **Note** If you click the icon that is blue at the bottom of the network list, the one the user is connected to, Wi-Fi is disabled. If a user can't connect to a network make sure he or she knows to click this icon to enable Wi-Fi. It could have been accidentally turned off.

Manage Wi-Fi Networks

If your users have had experience with Windows 8, they'll notice they are missing a few features. In Windows 8 users could right-click the networks shown to access other options, such as Forget this Network. That's no longer available. To manage networks in that manner, the user will need to access the Network and Internet options in Settings.

To access these settings:

1. Click Start and click Settings.

2. Click Network and Sharing.

3. Click Wi-Fi.

4. Click Manage Wi-Fi Settings.

5. Scroll down to Manage Wi-Fi Networks.

6. Click a network you've connected to. In Figure 7-21, I've selected a hotel network.

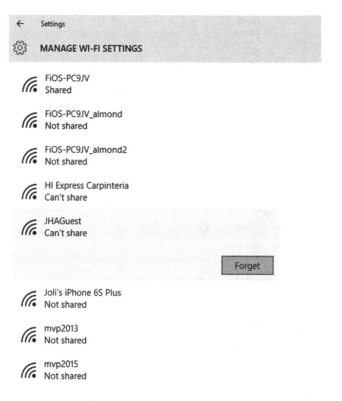

Figure 7-21. Select any network to forget it

7. Click Forget.

While you're here, click the Back arrow to return to the Network and Internet settings, and from Wi-Fi note that there are links to other areas of Windows where you can configure and manage networks. As shown in Figure 7-22, you can access the Network and Sharing Center here, change adapter settings, set up a HomeGroup, and more.

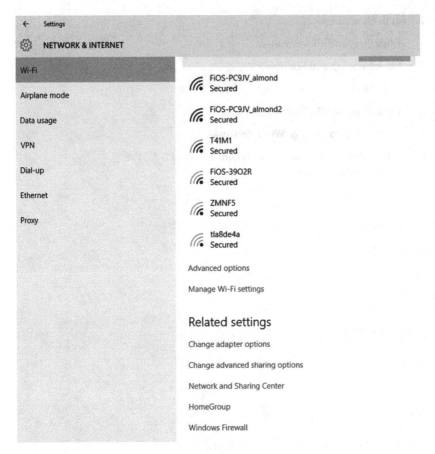

Figure 7-22. The Network and Sharing settings offers links to other network options

Network and Sharing Center

The Network and Sharing Center offers a more comprehensive, and possibly familiar, place to configure network settings. You can open this from the Network and Internet settings options shown earlier in Figure 7-22 or by right-clicking the Network icon on the Taskbar. Once you are there, notice these options, shown in Figure 7-23:

- View your active networks — to see if you are connected to a private, public, or domain network.

- Access type — to see if you are connected to the Internet or only a local network.

- Connection — to access the active connection to troubleshoot or view its properties.

- Set up a new connection or network — to configure a new connection, including VPNs.

- Troubleshoot problems — to access troubleshooting wizards to help resolve network problems.

- Change adapter settings — to see available network interface cards and view or manage their properties.

- Change advanced sharing options — to view settings for private, public, and domain networks. Access to these settings and others might be restricted by Group Policy.

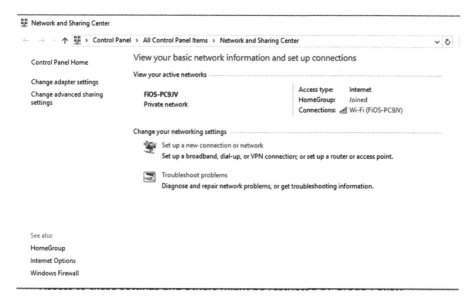

Figure 7-23. *Use the Network and Sharing Center to manage networks*

Troubleshoot Networks

For the most part, when problems arise, even if they are with networking, restarting the computer and reconnecting to the network is a good first step. And as with other operating systems, other viable solutions include updating device drivers, uninstalling and reinstalling network adapters, checking adapter settings, and so on. But for the average end users on a Windows To Go drive, perhaps the best place for them to start is to run the available Windows troubleshooters.

If problems arise with a network, users can access the troubleshooting wizards available by clicking Troubleshoot problems as shown in Figure 7-23. There, users can select from the following options. They can let Windows automatically troubleshoot:

- Internet Connections

- Shared Folders

133

- HomeGroup

- Network Adapter

- Incoming Connections

- Connections to a Workplace using DirectAccess

If running a wizard doesn't resolve the problem a user can click Change adapter settings to view more about the connected network (which they might discover is sending data but not receiving it, or vice versa). As you can see in Figure 7-24, a user might see lots of networks.

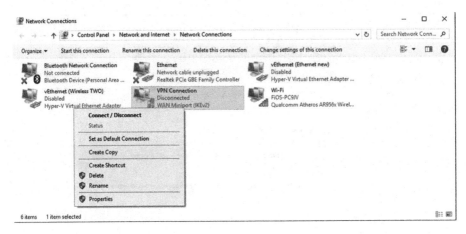

Figure 7-24. *Adapters are available by clicking Change adapter settings in the Network and Sharing Center*

Here there's a virtual private network, a wireless network, Bluetooth options, and even Ethernet options. There's also a Hyper-V adapter available. Users can right-click any network to connect or disconnect. Users can also click Properties to access additional information, such as their IP address or gateway.

Accounts

You saw earlier where you can access account options in Settings. I didn't go into much detail about account options there though. For the most part, with Windows To Go workspaces, users will use one of three account types: Local, Microsoft, and Domain.

A local account is an account that is only associated with the Windows To Go drive. The user profile is stored on the drive, and the profile exists only when the drive is in use. You can create a local account by clicking Start, Settings, Accounts, and then Your email and accounts. Figure 7-25 shows that I'm connected to this drive with a Microsoft account; thus, the option to sign in with a local account instead exists. To create a local account or switch to an existing one, click this link.

Figure 7-25. Switch accounts using the Accounts area of Settings

As you might expect, if you're signed in with a local account already the option to switch to one changes. (You can create additional local accounts as well.) It changes to Sign in with a Microsoft Account instead. A Microsoft account is another way to sign in. When you sign in with this kind of account you can access OneDrive from inside File Explorer, and your user profile is stored in the cloud. This means that as you log on to any other machine directly using the account, your profile follows you and is applied. This makes all of your computing sessions the same, because the user account is what applies settings like background, privacy, and so on each time you log on.

Finally, there's a domain account. You'll use a domain account to connect to your enterprise network. Users won't have much control over that account or settings associated with it; a domain administrator manages the account in the enterprise. Group Polices are applied when the user logs on too, and they often prevent the user from accessing or modifying system settings like the Firewall or Windows Defender, and Windows Updates, and might even prevent them from changing thing like screensavers and backgrounds.

File Explorer

File Explorer hasn't changed much over the years, except for the addition of the Ribbon and a link to OneDrive. Users might be thrown a little when they find out they can't right-click the Start button to get to it, but it's easy enough to access by clicking Start with the left mouse button. File Explorer can look like what's shown in Figure 7-26 on first use, but if you expand your favorite sections it'll look more like what's shown in 7-27. Teach your users how to get the most from File Explorer by teaching them this trick. I especially like Quick Access, as it offers links to the folders I use most often.

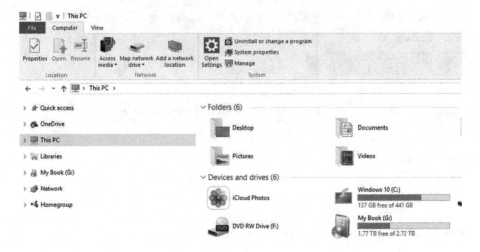

Figure 7-26. *File Explorer with nothing expanded in the left pane*

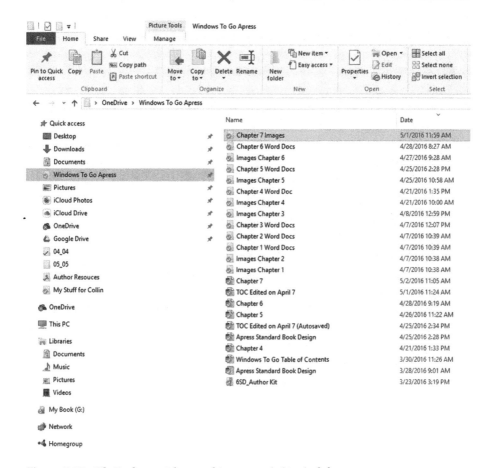

Figure 7-27. *File Explorer with everything expanded in the left pane*

If users incorporate OneDrive, iCloud, or Google Drive to store their documents, inform them there are links in File Explorer that work just like local folders. You can work inside these folders just like you would with any folder that's stored on the Windows To Go drive, and you can use the ribbon to do it. Make sure you let your users know that it's important to save any data they create using their Windows To Go drive either to the cloud or to a domain or local network share.

Summary

Windows 10 is quite a bit different from Windows 7 or 8/8.1 and it's important your users know about these changes prior to giving them a Windows To Go workspace. Make sure they know how to connect to networks, change personal settings, and use File Explorer so they can get the most possible out of their drive. Also let them know that Windows 10 is meant to unify desktop PCs, Windows tablets, and Windows smartphones with one interface, using one account and one operating system.

Index

© Joli Ballew 2016
J. Ballew, *Windows To Go*, DOI 10.1007/978-1-4842-2134-1

Get the eBook for only $5!

Why limit yourself?

Now you can take the weightless companion with you wherever you go and access your content on your PC, phone, tablet, or reader.

Since you've purchased this print book, we're happy to offer you the eBook in all 3 formats for just $5.

Convenient and fully searchable, the PDF version enables you to easily find and copy code—or perform examples by quickly toggling between instructions and applications. The MOBI format is ideal for your Kindle, while the ePUB can be utilized on a variety of mobile devices.

To learn more, go to www.apress.com/companion or contact support@apress.com.

Printed in the United States
By Bookmasters